WHAT ELSE YOU GOT?
Freelancing in Radio

Mary Saner

Published by Head to Wind Publishing
PO Box 74
Galena, MD 21635

ISBN 978-1-939632-07-4

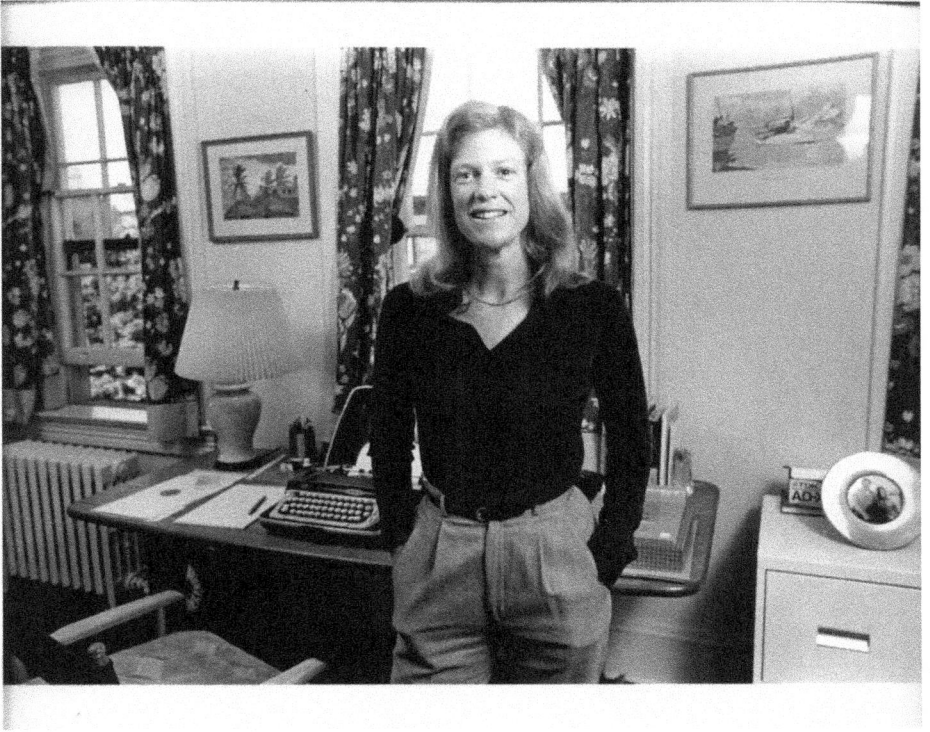

Photo courtesy of Bruce Reedy

To Buzz, Lucy and Leigh – my three favorite
voices

CONTENTS

Prologue

Some people know what profession they want to be in by the time they are nine. I didn't. I still have barely an inkling when I'm twenty-nine.

After college, with thoughts of becoming a teacher, I end up in New Orleans getting a Master's degree in history at Tulane University. Though I was falling in love with the town – its Dixieland jazz, oyster po'boys, and laid-back lifestyle – I head north towards Washington DC to pursue another serious interest. He becomes my husband not long after. In Washington, I study more history at George Washington University with hopes of an eventual PhD. Then one day while reading the university's newspaper, a job advertisement catches my eye. The Women's Athletics Department is looking for an assistant basketball coach to also help in promoting sports teams.

I love sports, so I apply. And I get the job. A year later, I'm the Women's Sports Information Director at GW. When announcing a women's college basketball game at GW, two students from a visiting team invite me to join their half-time radio show. I take a seat at the press table between the young men and put on the headphones. It's hard to explain what happens next but being in a charged atmosphere, and hearing my voice amplified in headphones while talking about something I'm interested in (basketball) is exciting. The broadcasters ask me lots of good questions. The show moves fast. I laugh a lot – don't remember what's so funny, only that I knew I'd like to try this again. I think I may have hit on what I truly want to do. This experience is enough to get me thinking about sportscasting as a possible career.

PART ONE

WFMD

AM 93

Idon't recall who first tells me about Bernard Adams, but once I hear his name it keeps coming up. Adams is considered one of the best news directors in the radio business. He runs an award-winning news department at a small station outside of Washington in Frederick, Maryland. He's also known for offering internships to people who have lots of interest but little or no experience in broadcasting – like me.

Arriving at WFMD for an interview, I find Adams downstairs in the newsroom. Had I known then of Samuel Jackson, I'd have seen the striking resemblance.

My meeting with Bernie Adams is nothing like routine. After a brief introduction, I'm reading news clippings for a voice test. He likes my voice and the way I read. He's not interested, though, in my questions about sportscasting. He doesn't need a sportscaster; he already has one. But if I'm interested in news work, he'll give me the internship. It will be three days a week for three months with no pay. Sounds good.

My internship begins right after New Year's 1983. I'll never forget the day. Bernie, who always looks stern except when he smiles, hands me a cassette tape recorder, shows me how to use it and sends me out to interview an official from a solar energy company that's expanding in town. He says to bring the tape back to the studio after the interview and write a short piece for a newscast. While I'd interviewed some student athletes at George Washington University, I'd never used a tape recorder or written a radio newscast.

The interview goes well. I think I have the information I need. All the way back to the station I'm thinking about how to write the piece. In the parking lot, I take out a pencil and the notepad Bernie gave me and start writing. Better to have some idea what the story will be before showing up in the newsroom and struggling with it. How long I'm in the car I'm not sure, but a lot of people drive by, and I'm not making any progress. Finally, I give up and go inside where I'm about to learn how to write for radio.

Most days I work with Bernie in his office, which is also a production studio and full of recording equipment. It's next door to the broadcast studio.

Watching Bernie at work is amazing. No matter where he is, he always answers the phone on the first ring. If in the next couple seconds, he hears a potential news story, he switches on his tape machine and tells the person that the conversation is being taped. (He says it really fast, but he says it.) Then he fires off questions. He's direct but not pushy. After the call, he transfers the best quotes or "sound bites" to a "cart" – a plastic cartridge containing a loop of tape that he can play during the broadcast. Finally, he writes the copy or script, which ties everything together. Bernie's copy is short and to the point. He lets whoever's interviewed tell the story, and he writes the text – what some writers call the "connective tissue" – around those sound bites. When Bernie sits down at the mic, switches it on and begins broadcasting, his newscast comes together seamlessly. Just his deep resonant voice says: "Listen up."

It's only a couple weeks into the internship when Bernie tells me I'll be going on the air the next day to broadcast news stories that his reporters, John Fieseler and Randy Gray, have written. It's strange: I'm not excited or scared; I feel numb. But I've been practicing reading news clips, so I feel ready. The next morning, I take a seat at the 'big board' (the audio console). It reminds me of the instrument panel in an airplane cockpit – lots of controls. I switch on the microphone, which at this stage is all I need to do. I'm set for my very first broadcast.

Richard C. Hottelet, the veteran CBS newsman, gives his national newscast right before mine. I'm listening to him. His voice is gripping. What would it take to sound like that? Some experience would probably help. When Richard C. Hottelet signs off, I'm on-air. It must have been a jolt for listeners to go from Mr. Hottelet to me, although they probably stayed tuned out of curiosity. I make it through the newscast with no major gaffes. What I recall most is relief at the end.

Every day there's something new. A couple of months into the internship, I learn a crucial lesson. It's St. Patrick's Day. Not being Irish or having any plans for celebrating, I'm not thinking at all about the holiday. Getting a late start driving to Frederick I get caught up in traffic. I'm scheduled to broadcast the news this morning, and arriving at the station late, I run downstairs to the studio and grab the news stories that Randy, John and Bernie have written and stacked next to the microphone. Several of the stories aired yesterday, but they're updated for today's early broadcasts. I always take time to read them before going on the air, but today I'm rushed.

Putting on the headphones I turn on the microphone and begin. I can't recall now Randy's exact words, but hear myself read something like… "In celebration of St. Patrick's Day tomorrow" (The tomorrow part I'm sure about.) By the time I finish the word "tomorrow," Bernie's standing next to me. Wow, he got in here fast from the production studio! I want to yell "Help!" but I'm still on the air. After a stupid comment about St. Patrick's Day, I sign off. Bernie has walked back to his office without saying anything. I'm too upset to say anything. But there's a sinking feeling in my stomach. What just happened is avoidable – amateurish. While Randy later apologizes for not changing "tomorrow" for "today," it shouldn't have mattered. There's a cardinal rule in radio: Always read the copy before going on-air with it!

Often, when there's a break from work, Bernie and I talk about sports. He's a big pro basketball fan and really likes Bill Walton – the 6'11" center with red hair, who attracts a lot of attention when he's on the court. Bernie never says why he's so high on Walton, who often plays injured and works as hard on defense as offense. But Bernie insists that no pro player is as good as Walton and when someone in the newsroom begs to differ, he just smiles and says quietly, "Walton."

Work is becoming fairly routine at the station. But then Bernie pops a big question. How would I like to produce a documentary for WFMD? He's already titled it: "Babies Having Babies." (Teenage Pregnancy in Frederick County). I should probably have taken a moment to think about this, but I don't. I say yes immediately.

From practically the moment he hands me a list of people to contact to the last days of my internship, I'm absorbed in this effort. The documentary ends up revolving around hours of interviews with caring people in Frederick. There are many, including two high school counselors. One of them is about to retire after twenty-five years and has much to say to parents. There's also the head of the County Health Department, who says contraceptives are not just for girls but who supports their distribution to boys. And then there are two teenagers, one who has become a mother at 15, the other at 16 and the 16-year-old's mom, who talk about anger and hurt and love and support. In a way, it's as though everyone is talking to one another – saying out loud things that need to be said – and then offering some advice – like how important it is to talk things out.

From the very start of work on the show, Bernie has wanted Michael Jackson's hit song "Billie Jean" to introduce the first part. The song is about a boy and a girl and a baby. "Be careful what you do…remember to always think twice," Jackson sings above an intense beat. It is a dramatic way to begin the documentary.

The documentary airs as a four-part series. I'm downstairs in the newsroom listening to the first segment when I look up and see John Fieseler standing on the stairway just staring at me. He doesn't say anything, then disappears back up the stairs. It's then that I know my documentary is good. The phones are

5

ringing as listeners are calling in to the station; Bernie wants me to host a call-in show. I should probably be thrilled with the idea. But I'm not. The thought of being live on the air with callers who may be upset, irritated or angry makes me uneasy. I'm thinking of the parts of the documentary dealing with birth control, distributing contraceptives, sex education and parental responsibility. But I don't say anything to Bernie. I don't want him to know how nervous I am. The call-in show never gets scheduled – not because I decline to host it, (I wouldn't have declined, no matter how nervous), but because my three-month internship has come to an end.

While I plead to stay on as a reporter, Bernie has a policy of never hiring his interns. But as I'm leaving WFMD, he hands me an audition tape of two of my newscasts with my documentary. He has saved it all on a reel and has labeled the reel so the tape won't get deleted and another recording put on it. On the label in huge letters, he's written: DO NOT ERASE OR YOU WILL BE TORTURED. There's also a letter of reference from him, which is worth a lot to me. I've got a great voice, he says, but have much to learn. I know it's true. I've only been in the radio business for three months. But he also writes that I'm mature. I think it's for this reason that he put me on the air so soon, and trusted me with documentary work. I've learned a lot from him – how to write for radio, how to put a newscast together and how to broadcast it. In this short, three-month period, he's taught me what I need to know to get a job in radio.

KIX COUNTRY

A friend in radio tells me about a job opening in Alexandria, Virginia at WPKX. "KIX Country," a Top 10 station in the Washington area, is looking for a reporter to anchor three broadcasts every afternoon during rush hour. It's a key time spot for a radio person. There are also three Saturday morning newscasts to anchor. News, traffic and weather reports make up the broadcasts. A lot of the information for these broadcasts comes from an Associated Press (AP) teletype machine that churns out national and international news day and night. The stories in the reports also cover some state and local news and sports, the stock market and interesting features. The stories are often long and packed with information. They need rewriting to make them easier for listeners to understand in a three-minute newscast. The job is a big step up from an internship, though it's one that a seasoned radio person wouldn't find too difficult. I'm excited to get an interview.

At the station, I meet KIX's news director, Paul Bottoms, for my interview. Bottoms sounds a lot like Paul Harvey whose inimitable news reports liven up the airwaves. Bottoms anchors the news during Morning Drive – the day's primetime for radio (6-10 am). While he knows I'm inexperienced, he likes my voice – now described as "smoky" (whatever that means). We go over the kinds of stories he wants in the newscasts. He wants the lead to always be a major news story and says not to use the same lead in consecutive newscasts. And to vary the length of stories, too.

"Don't use long ones back to back," he explains, "but drop a short piece [one or two sentences] in the middle. It gives the newscast some punch."

It's a short interview. He needs someone to start right away. I'm available. And I'm in.

I'm pretty nervous going into KIX that first day. Walking into the newsroom around noon, the teletype machine is cranking out a steady stream of paper filled with the news stories of the day. Tearing off sheets, I start reading – crime stories, unemployment figures, interest rates, reports on dangerous weather around the country. Some of the top stories have long, fact-filled versions as well as short, summarized ones. I choose four stories for my first newscast, grabbing the long versions. The more facts, the better I can understand the story and write it in my own words.

Now, what story should I lead with? What will be the lead sentence? I write a sentence, cross it out and write another. There's a stream of people coming into the newsroom to say hi and introduce themselves. People at KIX are really nice. I tell them I'll stop by their desk later to talk, when things aren't so frantic, and keep working. When I finally decide on the stories and where they'll fit into my newscast, I type them into a script, but the newscast still needs a taped weather forecast and a traffic report. Even though there should be plenty of time to pull everything together, I feel rushed – right up to the moment I walk into the broadcast booth.

It's bigger than a phone booth, but not much. I'm glad I'm not claustrophobic. Sitting down at the console, I switch on the microphone and get ready to broadcast. There's a hand-cue from the disk jockey. His finger's pointing at me. I'm on-air. "88 and sunny at 3:50, good afternoon, I'm Mary Saner, K-I-X News." In a few fast-moving minutes, I run through the news, traffic and weather, then sign off. I take a deep breath. Then the phone in the booth rings. *That's fast*, I'm thinking. Picking up, I hear Paul's voice. There's no greeting just "Mary don't lead with that story." My heart drops. We'd gone over what kinds of stories make good leads. A lead should be a big, overriding story – the most important thing, what a person wants to know first, what affects them the most. It could be about war, jobs, food, gasoline or home prices, an airline strike. Unfortunately, my lead was about personnel changes at NPR. Another lesson learned.

In the next month, I master some fundamentals quickly, like when to use acronyms for organizations, for example, never to say Government Employees Insurance Companies – just GEICO. Paul jokes that even people who work there don't know what the letters stand for. Picking stories for newscasts is getting easier, partly because I learn the demographic. KIX listeners are mostly between 25 and 54 and live in the Washington area – northern Virginia, suburban Maryland and D.C. Many work for the government. And they like country music stars like Kenny Rogers, Dolly Parton, Kris Kristofferson and Crystal Gayle, who once in a while we'll mention in an entertainment piece.

Paul always leaves copies of his morning newscasts on the desk for me to read when I get to the station. They show me how he's reporting stories. Paul's copy is always easy to read and understand because our listeners need a very straight forward report – it's all taken in in one shot. They can't go back and reread to clarify. Paul never wastes a word and is an expert at boiling a story down for our listeners so it's just the essence. It's extremely effective. When reporting on Marvin Gaye's death, Paul uses two short sentences – Gaye's father shot him. There was bad blood. In two vivid sentences, he's said what happened and why.

Paul also leaves me notes on ways to improve newscasts – like not making everything sound like a crisis. He writes, "I don't want every story we do to be at the same shouting level because when a big story comes along, then we have no way of differentiating that from a small story."

Paul's pet peeve is using words and phrases that he says have been beaten to death like: it remains to be seen; on again, off again; crystal clear; oil-rich Middle East; last but not least; and back to the drawing board. The one he hates the most is "packing winds."

"What does that mean?" he asks me. I'm trying to explain it, but before I can he says, "Don't use it!"

Roger. Got it!

On the news desk one Friday afternoon, there's a piece of AP wire copy Paul has left for me. My documentary on teen pregnancy has won a regional award for Best Documentary from the Associated Press. I haven't mentioned it to Paul, but Bernie had called earlier to tell me the piece won both AP and UPI awards. I didn't even know it was submitted for an award, so this is a big surprise. Yes! I may have finally found what I'm really good at. Bernie sounded happy. While he's used to getting awards, I don't know how many involved interns. I'm already thinking about the awards ceremony in Rehoboth Beach, Delaware. Bernie will be there and, probably, some other radio friends.

I'd like to celebrate this Friday night, but that's not such a good idea. I need to be at the station tomorrow morning to do three newscasts beginning at 5:50, which means I need to get up at 3:20AM. I'm not even remotely an early riser. It's always a struggle for me. So, to make sure I get up, I buy another alarm clock that sounds like a fire alarm and set it to go off ten minutes after the first one. And it works. But even though I'm up and moving, it takes a little longer for my brain to kick in at full throttle. On these mornings, it's hard to process information. But at least on Saturday, fewer listeners are tuned in so the pressure is off a bit. Walking into the newsroom at that hour and seeing the reams of Associated Press (AP) that have streamed out of the teletype machine all night and fallen into piles on the floor doesn't feel quite as overwhelming as it might on a weekday.

I'm actually getting into a routine and think I'm fine with the early morning demands until one Saturday morning broadcast. At first it seems like others I've done. I run through the news and end with: "The weather is next on K.I.X." Then I push a button that activates the tape of a 30-second commercial. I listen for a moment to make sure the tape is playing. I close my eyes for just an instant. It feels SOOO good. The next thing I know, Bam! I'm lifting my head off the microphone. And it's time to read a short weather report. My heart's thumping so loud I'm hoping listeners can't hear it! There's a script still in my hand. I get through the weather – and the rest of the broadcast.

Unlike Saturday mornings when I get the weather forecast from the AP wire, every weekday afternoon before my first broadcast, I call weatherman Earl Finckle in Chicago. He's friendly and funny and usually accurate in his broadcasts. I tape him voicing two separate but similar weather forecasts for my three upcoming newscasts. I use one of them in my first and last newscast and the other in between so listeners won't hear the same forecast hour after hour and get bored with it. Earl is syndicated – his reports are carried in radio stations all over the country. But his listeners don't know it. They all think he's in their hometown. One afternoon the tape's rolling and Earl's giving me the forecast. He starts talking about the sunny, beautiful day we're having when I interrupt.

"Earl, it's raining here – really lousy."

There's a pause. I can hear him thinking. He begins again – "mostly cloudy with showers this afternoon…"

I'm laughing pretty hard at this point. Luckily, I'm just taping and am not on air.

I'm not sure how many stations carry Earl's forecasts but my mother-in-law in Springfield, Illinois tunes in to him and says he's her favorite weatherman. She likes his folksy, cheerful manner. But Paul, for whom brevity is the soul of radio, is not as much a fan as my mother-in-law. In Paul's opinion, Earl goes off the track too much and is too wordy. Paul gives me an example by taping a recent forecast when Earl says, "We've got ourselves a partly cloudy, windy and much cooler, highly refreshing day shaping up for today, go out and get 'em." Paul thinks it would be better just to say "windy and much cooler today."

Since Paul's not around in the afternoons to talk with Earl, he asks me to talk with him. For one thing, he says to tell Earl not to give a five-day forecast – it's too much information. But Earl likes to give an extended forecast. It's part of his routine. And it's hard to change old and successful habits. Paul keeps insisting on Earl changing the routine – and Earl keeps giving his extended forecast. There's another taped forecast that's got all the originality and personal touch that my mother-in-law likes, but which drives Paul crazy. On the transcript, Paul underlines what he doesn't like, which begins right after Earl's lead-in with the deejay.

"Well, Jim, <u>hang on to your keys to the cabin or any other summer paraphernalia you have because</u> after this little cool snap we've had over the weekend a big fat warm up is going to get underway. We see readings heading back into at least the 80's and <u>you know, don't tell anybody,</u> 90 is a possibility before this week is over <u>on a gusty southerly wind</u>. As of today, <u>let's get going onto</u> partly cloudy, no or little increase in clouds, <u>I'll give you your choice</u>. The temperature will be headed up to about 67 degrees and there will be a chance of a widely scattered shower or thundershower and thunderstorms will end early and clear to partly cloudy to clearing, low down to 53. Sunshine returns tomorrow. We head for 76…and why don't you come with me on Wednesday and go for a high of 80 sunshiny degrees."

Paul's not happy. He tells me to have Earl re-do any forecasts that are confusing. Of course, that doesn't mean Earl will. He has a formula for success, he's syndicated, and Paul's not his boss. But as time passes, Earl's forecasts seem less irritating to Paul, or maybe Paul's just getting used to Earl. Whatever it is, there's less complaining and I don't need to talk to Earl about it again.

Sometimes the wire services have offbeat features in their feeds. They're marked "kickers." Once in a while I use one in my last broadcast on Friday afternoon, thinking that if it makes me laugh, it may make listeners laugh as we go into the weekend. There's a story that catches my eye one Friday about a college course on kissing. Gold. I snatch it off the wire, rewrite it and type it into my script.

On the air, I move through three serious stories. Then comes the kissing one. Reading along, I'm thinking "is this funny…is anyone laughing?" I'm sitting in a booth alone without a laugh track or an audience that can let me know if this is working. Now, nearly at the end – SMACK! Then another lip-smacking sound. Oh Brother! Our disk jockey, John, is listening. And offering feedback! We both laugh and cut to a commercial. Paul tells me later that he liked the kissing story.

Paul's going on vacation and says I'll be taking over his morning news shift. It won't be anything like Saturday mornings when I do three newscasts. Instead, there'll be nine broadcasts – six news, two sports, and a taped health report – all before 8:30 am! The place is awash in paper that gets tossed around these mornings. It covers the desk and floor. The place looks like a small typhoon swept through.

I'll be working with a new disk jockey from Cleveland, Gary Dee, who hosts the morning drive. Gary is ahead of his time in local radio. He's provocative, controversial; he stirs up the emotions of listeners. He reminds me of the shock jock, Howard Stern. Now it's Gary who is often the topic of conversation around the station. Seems like everyone is talking about something outrageous he's just said. Not having worked Paul's daily morning shift before, I haven't been on the air with Gary and heard his show, so I have no idea that I've been featured in it. Paul tells me that Gary has given Earl the nickname "Captain" and is saying things like: "The Captain is busy chasing Mary Saner around the newsroom." It would be a feat for Earl to be able to do that since he's several states away. The whole thing is ridiculous but it gets some laughs on Gary's show.

Paul hasn't told me anything about working with Gary, but in my first few mornings on the job, I'm finding him easy to work with. One morning Gary leads into my newscast talking about an old song that he's just played.

"Mary, do you remember that one?" he asks.

"Gary, I'm not that old." The words slip out of my mouth.

The second I say it, I think Oh no! I just insulted our older listeners who happen to know the song. In a split second, Gary says something like, 'Mary we're all getting older...'

'We're not getting any younger...' I respond.

We move quickly into the news.

Working the morning shift is tough even with two alarm clocks. Friends who've worked mornings for a long time tell me that it never gets easier, that they never really adjust. They just cope with the lack of sleep. My husband is not on my 0-dark-hundred wake-up schedule. And it doesn't help that I can't get to sleep until about three hours before I have to get up. After two weeks of the morning rush, Paul's back from vacation and I can't wait to get back to afternoon news.

One afternoon I'm pulling together a newscast when the phone rings. I always pick up the same way.

"Newsroom."

"Hi Mary. It's Bill" says the voice at the other end.

"Who's Bill?" I'm wondering.

Fact is, I don't know Bill – but Bill knows me. He's a KIX listener who's about to give me a tip. Inside his car, driving on a section of the Shirley Highway in suburban Virginia, our listening area, Bill says traffic is moving now that the accident has been cleared. That's a change from the most recent traffic report off the wire, which reported a bottleneck there. I use Bill's update in my upcoming newscast. Sometimes when reading newscasts, I wonder who's listening and what they're thinking or saying. People like Bill occasionally let me know and help me update the news at the same time. I like it when they call in.

While I like working with Paul and others at KIX, I keep thinking about producing features and documentaries – about the chance to connect with more people, dig deeper into a subject, interview, write and produce shows. There isn't much of an opportunity here – unlike my documentary work at WFMD. When a programming shake-up ends the afternoon news and weather at KIX, I leave. It's time to try producing on my own.

FREELANCING

Ah, the freedom of freelancing! Freedom to come up with offbeat, unusual ideas, freedom to find editors that are easy to work with, freedom to work at my own pace and without deadlines. It's finding new ideas for radio features that isn't so easy. Networks like NPR may have a hundred or more correspondents around the country looking for new stories. I need to find that interesting piece that no one else has found and find the right place to sell it.

Buying a Sony tape recorder with a shoulder strap and a hand-held microphone is a first step. I chose it because a friend has told me about riding his motorcycle down the highway with his Sony strapped to the back of the bike. In a curve, the recorder flies off, bounces off the pavement and tumbles down a hill. When he finds the recorder and turns it on, it works fine. Good news for any durability concerns. I'm sold.

Not long after, I get the chance to record some interviews with athletes with my new equipment and to sell those interviews to a station or network.

At an old church in Washington DC where the basement has been turned into a training room for boxers, I meet up with welterweights Simon Brown and Maurice Blocker, both 23 and close friends, who are training here. Simon's record as a professional boxer is 22-1 with 16 knockouts. He's short, muscular and talkative and tells me he'd only fight his friend if it's in a title match. But he always tries to knock out his opponent. Maurice is tall, thin and soft spoken, and 22-0 in his boxing career. As for training in a church?

"You have to watch your language," says Maurice, who apparently doesn't mind doing that. "Church is a lovely place to be – even in the boxing world."

Having recorded interviews and also the sounds of a trainer yelling, fists hitting bags, and boxers talking – the potential background sound for the piece – I call KMOX Radio in St. Louis. I've heard there's a fellow there named Bob Costas who has a syndicated sports show. It airs on 400 stations. Bob answers the phone. He's nice, asks me a few questions about my tape, then tells me to send something on. I don't think Bob Costas uses any of my tape, but his interest and willingness to listen to my pitch and the sound I sent him still stands out in my mind as encouraging. It spurs me on.

MALL WALKING

I'm brainstorming a lot with my friend, Sandy Zimmet, who interned before me at WFMD. I got to know Sandy when she'd stop by the station to say hi to Bernie. She's now a freelance news reporter for Washington-area stations. When Sandy and I get an idea, we often run it by Bernie. His trademark response is: "What else you got?" Knowing that's what he'll say, we usually have at least two other ideas. But it's my sister in Connecticut who comes up with the idea that turns into my first feature story.

In a phone call, she tells me about a new health trend in America that she's heard about from our aunt in Los Angeles. It's called mall walking. Mall walking is gaining popularity with men and women alike who want to get exercise year-round in a controlled environment. As far as I can tell, no mall walking story has ever been done. This will be the first, an important point for a freelancer selling a piece.

I line up an interview with Dr. Samuel Fox, who's the director of the Preventive Cardiology program at Georgetown University. Dr. Fox is relaxed and talkative and tells me that walking is one of the healthiest exercises people can do since it improves circulation. He says he writes prescriptions for exercise, and he's been recommending mall walking to heart patients for fifteen years.

There's a mall in Wheaton, Maryland, a northern suburb of Washington. Walkers come in Monday, Wednesday and Friday mornings at 8:30 before the mall opens and walk for an hour. Not just seniors but people of all ages join the mall walking program, the Rise and Shine Club, which is free.

Whenever I arrive at the scene of a story, I always record two or three minutes of the sounds of the place. It's called "ambience." Here, it's of people walking by and music playing on the mall sound system. I'll use this sound later on when producing the program. Dropping it in at different places adds color and helps put the listener where the story is taking place.

I get a lot of exercise taping this show. It's a quarter of a mile around the indoor course at Wheaton Plaza, and I complete it several times while holding up a microphone and recording fast moving walkers. Only once do I think I might pass out and have to sit down to catch my breath. There's a Red Cross booth on the course for anyone who needs help, but I'm not at that stage — yet!

Walkers tell me that in the mall they don't have to worry about lighting or traffic or barking dogs, that there's no pollen or exhaust fumes or hills to climb. It's just smooth, easy walking. One woman says it's fun meeting people and talking with them while exercising.

About two hundred people have joined the Rise and Shine Club. In addition to the benefits the walkers gain, the Mall's marketing director, Anne Korff, says many of them give her helpful advice about everything from floor wax to mall exhibits.

My program ends up being three minutes long. NPR edits and buys the show. It's for "Morning Edition." I've listened to "Morning Edition" with host Bob Edwards for the past year and am somewhat in awe of him. When I walk past him at NPR's studio in Washington, I think about stopping to introduce myself, but lose my nerve and instead just say hi. He says hi back.

But a few days later on "Morning Edition," Bob reads the introduction to my show ending it in a slow, deliberate way. "What they do is called mall walking," he says in his signature drawl. Wow. That sets the piece up! My sister, Ginny, is listening to the program at home in Connecticut and calls me at the end of it.

"It's terrific!" she says.

She has my mother and father tuned in as well. I'm riding pretty high on this day. I'd gotten there first with this idea. It's not until a year later that Time magazine publishes an article on mall walking. I'm surprised it took so long.

In the next year, I take on five features for NPR — all are 'on spec' (speculative) stories. That means that NPR is interested when I pitch my ideas but makes no commitment to air or pay for the pieces, so I do them in hopes they'll be sold. Part and parcel of the freelance life. But the network ends up buying and airing all of them, which adds to my credentials as well as my bank account. I produce several other shows on spec for The Christian Science Monitor Radio and for Mutual Broadcasting System. The stories range from fish migration to bobsledding to Philippe Petit. I think I'm onto something!

PEACE CUP

I have to get to the scene of a story in order to do the story. It doesn't come to me. On this hot summer day, I get lost driving to a soccer tournament on the northeast side of Baltimore. Driving back and forth on the same streets for a half hour, I get panicky, then hit a speed bump going too fast and crunch my front bumper. Part of it falls off and drags along the road. I turn onto a quiet street and stop to try and fix it when a man walks over and offers to help. His truck is parked in a nearby driveway. Grabbing a toolbox out of the back of the truck, he lies down on the pavement in front of my car and goes to work fixing my bumper. I'm chattering away, thanking him over and over again while telling him how lost I am looking for this soccer field.

"I know the field," he says. "I'm going there to see the games. You can follow me."

The part luck plays in radio!

After fixing my bumper, the man and his kids, who have gathered to watch the car repair show on the street in front of their house, jump in the truck. I follow them all to the park.

The tournament features four teams made up of teenage boys – Iraqi, Burmese, Bhutanis, and Meskhetian Turks (a Turkish-speaking Muslim minority group deported by Stalin in the 1940's). The boys are all refugees whose families have come to escape their war-torn countries. Soccer has brought them together.

Between games the kids talk to me about what they have left behind. There was no chance to play soccer or do much of anything else in his country, an Iraqi boy tells me.

"It's too dangerous. We cannot live there. We don't have jobs. We cannot study. There's war, there's shooting, there are guns, gangs, the army, fighting between people. Here's better for us – safe."

The International Rescue Committee has sponsored the tournament, which is called the Peace Cup. (One of my daughters eventually interns with this terrific organization). Along the sidelines family and friends, including the kind man, who helped me with my car, and his family, cheer the teams on. I ask a team member, who's watching from the sidelines with his foot atop a soccer ball, to show me some of his skills.

"Like what?" he says.

16

"Anything."

And, it's Showtime! The ball flips up and around his foot like it's attached by a string. All I can do is laugh.

Lugging my equipment around the soccer field, stopping to tape interviews with players, fans and officials, taping ambience of whistles and cheers, and snapping pictures of the whole scene is taking a toll on me. I'm wilting in the sun. During times of fatigue like this one, I count on adrenaline to carry me through. But it's been a long day with the drive, then getting lost, then car troubles, and now doing the story. Since I arrived late for the games, I figure it's better not to sit down in the grass and rest but instead, finish up my work before the tournament ends. A fellow on the sidelines, who had spoken to me earlier about how hard I'm working, asks if he can help by carrying something. I've got the recorder strapped over my shoulder and the mic and camera in hand. But my equipment bag — a leather Amish carrying case with lots of zippered pockets — is heavy with extra equipment. It's a nice gesture on his part, and I thank him, but I'm almost done.

Gathering sound is what I like best about radio feature work. While it can be exhausting, it's highly rewarding. I love going back and listening to all the tape, all the voices, and deciding how to use the sound to tell the story.

My show is for Voice of America. During the interviews, I ask people to respond to questions first in English and then in their native language, something VOA editors told me to do when I first started. Though I always remember, they remind me when I'm interviewing people whose native language is not English. Since the program will air around the world, there will be no need to translate the sound bites in countries where their language is spoken.

Produced for Voice of America

PHILIPPE PETIT

Usually, I don't try to interview people who have agents or managers. That's because they're already well known; their story has been told or is continually being told. But Philippe Petit's an exception to my rule. He has an exciting, ongoing story. Having now done some freelance work for two networks, I'm feeling pretty confident about contacting famous people for interviews, so I call his manager and arrange for an interview in New York City where Petit is living.

Petit has already walked on a high wire between the Trade Towers and is preparing to walk an inclined wire from the floor to the ceiling of the Cathedral of St. John the Divine in New York. It's the 100th Anniversary of St. John's – the largest Gothic cathedral in the world. The event is being called a high wire concert since concert pianist Evelyn Crochet will play while Petit climbs.

I meet Petit in a building in downtown Manhattan. His young daughter is with him. She's on the move – pretending to walk the tightrope. Standing on a wide indoor window sill, she slowly puts one foot in front of the other, imitating her father. Then she steps up onto a long radiator cover and continues her high wire act. Her father lets her play while we talk.

"The wire to me is not a place to challenge the audience but to inspire them," the wiry, intense Frenchman tells me, "so I'm not interested in being a dancer like in the circus, faking falls. I'm interested in the easiness, simplicity, purity of something so easy everyone could do it walking on a high wire."

Petit has a sense of humor. He talks about being careful so he can live to be very old and do many projects. I'm thinking how the word "careful" takes on a whole new meaning in his line of work. With all the concentration that's needed to walk on a wire, Petit says there is no room for fear – not until afterwards.

"When I finish a performance, that's where I look back at what I did. Very often I'm frightened at what I've done. I say, Wow, I went a little bit too far on this one!"

While he has probably done lots of interviews, Petit hasn't lost his enthusiasm for them. The love for his work comes through in the passion in his voice. Up to now I've produced only seven feature stories, so am still pretty new at the job. Follow-up questions aren't as obvious to me. I'm not as focused and am spending too much time worrying about background noise and whether my recorder's working right. Petit tells me he has had one serious accident walking the wire, and that it changed him.

It happened, he says, in 1975 just as he was about to join a one-year tour with Ringling Brothers and Barnum & Bailey Circus. While not critically injured in the fall, Petit calls it "a lesson from destiny."

"It put wise blood into the vein," he says, "I know I can't fall anymore."

I wish I'd asked him about the accident, how it happened and more about how it changed him.

My three-minute feature on Petit ends up on Mutual's early news show called "America in the Morning."

LOOKING FOR IDEAS IN ALL THE ODD PLACES

Fresh ideas are a freelancer's bread and butter. I'm finding program ideas in the magazine section at bookstores. Obscure periodicals cover a lot of interesting and unusual subjects. There might be only a paragraph, but it can trigger a story idea. When visiting small towns, I try and stop in at the library and read the local paper. If a story idea interests me, I'll phone the person featured in the article, then decide whether to try to find a network to commission me for a piece.

Occasionally I take my radio equipment along on vacation. On a summer fly fishing trip to southwestern Montana, my husband, Buzz, and our fishing guide, Bill Saunders, plan a trip down the Madison River in Bill's 14-foot fiberglass boat. The Madison flows north, unlike most American rivers that flow south.

I've come along on the float to tape a feature story on catch and release fishing. At the time, it isn't common for people to catch and release fish. Worries about rivers being fished out aren't as widespread, so the story idea is pretty new.

Sitting in the stern of Bill's boat, I hold my recorder and microphone – ready to move into action at any moment. Buzz is standing and leaning into the bow. From there he has a wide view of the river ahead and can cast his dry fly, called a "hopper" (a grasshopper imitation) off either side of the boat. Bill, who's wearing a toothy grin and a fishing cap covering a mop of brown hair, sits in the middle seat gripping the oars and steering as we drift downstream. We're planning on a 12-mile float – most of it through water that is designated catch-and-release.

I lean forward and direct my microphone towards Bill.

"Okay, Buzz, we're going to be fishing down this bank – off to the left side. All the fish are going to be set fairly tight. Cast close. Any of these flat areas behind rocks – lay your fly in there. Nice cast!"

Buzz's fly lands in an eddy behind a large rock. The hopper sits up on the water looking like it just fell off the rock. I steal a few glances at the scenery around us. It's beautiful this August day – clear blue sky, mountains on both sides of the river with some of the tops still covered in snow.

Bill says he's been guiding on the Madison River for sixteen years.

"When I first started floating this river, the river was dying. People — outfitters and guides — were taking fish out faster than it would regenerate itself. So, it was literally dying. The guiding industry, floating industry, noticed this and started clamoring to the Fish and Game about how our river was dying, and they took notice and implemented some new programs, and it's come a long way back."

Stumbling up into the bow I point my mic towards Buzz as he casts his fly and watches it float downstream.

"You see anything out there?" I ask.

"I see a lot of clever fish out there avoiding my fly," he laughs. Then…Wham!

"Oh, big rainbow, nice jump!" Bill yells as Buzz jerks his fishing rod up and snags a trout. "That fish is about 14-15 inches, nice fish. Man, when he came out of the water, he wanted that hopper bad! Keep his head up. Bring him over to the boat and we'll get that net on him."

It's exciting seeing the fish close up, swimming near us. I can't help but cheer. "Boy, he bends that rod, doesn't he? What colors. Nice beautiful fish, Buzz!"

Bill moves the net towards the trout and scoops it up headfirst. Lifting it out of the net, he takes the hook out quickly but gently — careful not to tear the fish's mouth. For a split second while Bill holds it loosely in his hand, Buzz and I get to admire this beautiful fish glistening silver with a pink rainbow-like stripe along its body from gill to tail. Then holding it underwater, facing the swift current and an explosion of oxygen, Bill opens his hand. In a flash, the fish is gone. Everything has happened quickly. I'm wide-eyed.

"You get 'em in and out pretty fast."

"Yeah, that way you don't stress them out too much," says Bill.

Bill tells us that catch and release has been in effect on the Madison River for thirteen years. And now, as a result, there are about two thousand trout per mile in this stretch of river.

I record a lot of sound on this day — water splashing against the boat; oars creaking in the oarlocks and pushing through the waves, and Buzz and Bill talking. Much of it isn't used in my two-and-a half minute program for Mutual Broadcasting's "America in The Morning," but I always want to have too much sound rather than not enough. What tape is used captures the excitement of spending a day on one of the best trout fishing rivers in America.

NEW AND OFFBEAT

I'm starting to get the hang of producing features that are two to six minutes long. There's a rhythm to it. Not only do the shows need to catch the interest of listeners, but also put them where the story is taking place and tell them something new.

At the Walter's Art Gallery in Baltimore, an exhibit called "Artful Deception: The Craft of the Forger" just opened. The Museum's Curator of Medieval Art, Gary Vikan, has gathered paintings, sculpture, silver and jewelry for the show. In one room of the exhibit he has placed forged works alongside identical, genuine ones. Then he asks museum goers to identify which is the original and which is the fake. A wall text gives clues for helping people decide. Then viewers can lift up a flap on the wall to check their choices. The show brings in crowds of people who enjoy playing detective. Vikan tells me that common sense goes a long way in detecting a forgery. For example, a limestone head supposedly sculpted in the 4th century that has a nose perfectly intact would be suspicious. All those centuries with no damage is too hard to believe. I sell this feature to The Christian Science Monitor Radio.

While an unusual, interesting idea propels a feature, it's the interviews that are key to the show's success.

Recording them can be as easy as holding up a microphone between tennis superstars Boris Becker and Guillermo Vilas at a charity event in Washington – or as difficult as stumbling around Bill Saunders' boat trying to tape my husband, who's fishing and Bill, who's rowing, netting and releasing fish. But one thing is always the same. It is always the people I'm interviewing who tell the story. I'm not in it. I introduce them and provide some facts, but they carry the piece. As for interviewing Boris Becker and Guillermo Vilas – here's what happens.

A TENNIS TRIUMVIRATE

I t's always the hottest week of the summer, that third week in July, when the Washington Star newspaper sponsors a pro tennis tournament in Washington DC. Heat notwithstanding, thousands of fans turn out. Being an avid tennis player, I'm often in the stands watching many of the top players in the world competing. A family friend and neighbor who's an agent for several of the players arranges for me to talk with Boris Becker and Guillermo Vilas while they're at a benefit for the Special Olympics. In a large, crowded conference room, I stand with my recorder strapped over my shoulder, holding up my microphone between Becker, the 18-year-old strawberry blond superstar from Germany, who smiles a lot, and Vilas, a serious, soulful Argentinian. Both men prefer to talk about life off the tennis court. Guillermo, an extraordinary tennis player, who at one time ranked second in the world, tells me he loves poetry and music.

"I'm trying to make a record," he says. "I wrote the tunes, wrote the lyrics. Almost done. I will try to do it in English if I get better. So far in Spanish, I'm doing pretty well."

Vilas who speaks five languages (Portuguese, Italian, French, Spanish and English) says a love of art runs in his family. But he still wants to get back into tennis's Top Ten and says he's working hard to make it happen. I move my mic over to Boris, who has not yet become the top tennis player in the world, although he is the youngest man ever to win Wimbledon. Boris tells me he started playing tennis before he was six and loves the game so much he plays on vacations.

"What else do you like to do?" I ask.

"I like to go shopping in big cities and walk in the streets of New York. I love the United States," he says. "I like the easy way of life here. It's not so complicated here. You can do what you want."

Becker and Vilas share the same manager, Ion Tiriac, who's from Romania and was once a champion tennis player himself.

"I'm not very sophisticated," Tiriac tells me. "You have to do the same thing every day. I slowly try to retire – may go into the press or do some television."

Tiriac will become a businessman in Romania whose net worth is estimated at more than a billion dollars!

KEYS TO INTERVIEWING

No interview is exactly the same as another, but even so there are things I always do to prepare for them. Before every interview I jot down some questions and keep them in my mind. When meeting the person I'm going to interview, I always try and talk about a different subject than the one we'll be discussing in the interview. That way when the recorder is on and the tape's rolling, their answers won't sound rehearsed and stale, which can happen when people repeat information. Also, I tell the person that we're not live and that it's very informal. If the atmosphere isn't already relaxed, it is then.

Many of my stories take place outdoors. Since outdoor sounds like cars and people talking can be caught on tape – at a time when I don't want them to be – I try and find a quiet place to record. The same goes for avoiding indoor sounds like phones ringing and air conditioners going on and off. I recall interviewing a scientist inside a laboratory building and noticing a humming noise from the fluorescent lights overhead. Unfortunately, I ignore it. When playing the tape back, a distracting faint hum can be heard under the entire interview.

One of the most important things I've found in interviewing is to listen carefully to what is being said, and when there's an obvious follow-up question, ask it. Also, during an interview, I continually check the gauge or meter on the recorder to make sure sound is being recorded at the right level. Recording a voice too soft creates hissing on the tape and recording too loud distorts the voice.

If the person being interviewed wants to say something off the record, I turn the recorder off – or if I'm asked not to use a remark previously recorded, I don't use it. (If it's a potentially good sound bite, I may try to change their mind, but never push it.) As for the best time to ask the toughest question? For me, it's at the end of the interview. That way if the person is uncomfortable with the subject and doesn't want to answer, I can just turn off the recorder – the interview is over. In the course of an interview, rapport and trust can develop that makes tough questions less threatening. Asking the toughest question early on can put the person on their guard, making them less comfortable and open.

Interviewing gets easier over time. Sometimes during an interview, I hear an answer that I know I'll use in my piece. I'm hoping the recorded sound of it is clear. I may stop the interview, rewind the tape and listen just to make sure.

I always ask the same question at the end of an interview: "Is there anything else — anything we may have missed that you think listeners would want to know?" More often than not, the answer to that question becomes a key sound bite in the feature.

Interviews often require problem solving. I recall the woman who brought along her eight-month-old baby to one. He's adorable, all smiles, and settles into his stroller seeming content to watch his mother and me talking on the sofa a few feet away. Then begins a loudening chorus of gurgling and hiccupping — not ideal background sound for a show unrelated to babies. I don't want his mother to know he's a problem. She's relaxed — why make her uncomfortable?

My old leather jacket is beside me on the sofa — cords hanging down from both ends of the collar. I push it over to him. He grabs a cord, tugs on it, jiggles it, flings it — but without uttering a sound. I keep on with the questions to his mother while moving the other cord into position. Still no noise — and that's the way it is all the way to the end of the interview when I take the cords out of his tiny hands. Then comes a mighty scream. I credit my jacket with saving that interview!

I try not to get distracted while interviewing, but sometimes it's impossible. One experience especially comes to mind. It's a story for Mutual Broadcasting.

I'm interviewing a woman who's a founder of the American Bat Conservation Society. She's an authority on bats — very smart lady. In the interview, she tells me that bats have a bad image but that they are not aggressive; that they can eat 600 mosquitoes in an hour and that their droppings can be used as fertilizer. While she's talking, I notice her sleeve moving all the way up her arm. Yikes! I'm trying to concentrate on what she's saying when a bat pokes its head out from inside her collar. It's on her shoulder. The woman smiles and starts telling me all about this two-and-a-half inch long, brown bat that she's named "Sweet Pea." She found the bat on the ground when it was a baby and orphaned with its umbilical cord still attached. Sweet Pea was having trouble keeping its body temperature up so the woman kept her inside her shirt, taking her out every ten or fifteen minutes to feed her.

"She got used to that as being the place she'd prefer to be for the rest of her life — inside my shirt," she explains. "There she goes," she laughs, as Sweet Pea disappears back down her sleeve.

"What does it feel like?" I ask.

"It's kind of like wearing fur inside your shirt and occasionally the fur moves," she replies.

The bat has been vaccinated against rabies. But she tells me never to pick up a bat or any wild animal. Then she asks me if I want to hold Sweet Pea. I don't, but before I can answer she hands her over. It's amazing looking in the bat's mouth at a row of tiny bottom teeth that looks like a miniature saw blade – most effective for eating all those insects. I'm happy to hand Sweet Pea back!

Everything about this interview is odd except the person I'm interviewing. She's knowledgeable, articulate and sensible, which needs to come through or the show is no longer a science piece. Humor is effective as long as it doesn't overwhelm, as long as there's balance.

In this case, getting good ambience for the show proves difficult since bats don't make sounds audible to humans. If Sweet Pea were a bird, well, that's a different story.

THE BRITS

Sometimes in radio you get lucky and find a story within a story. It happens to me on the Appalachian Trail. Over the years I've usually lived within an easy drive of the Appalachian Trail (aka the A.T.) and have walked different sections of it. One of the prettiest and rockiest stretches I've hiked is in south central Pennsylvania. Here I discovered Pine Grove Furnace, an important stopover place for thru-hikers, those who walk the entire Trail – 2,000 miles.

Pine Grove Furnace in Gardners, PA marks the halfway point on the Trail, which stretches from Georgia to Maine. When thru-hikers stop at the General Store, they're awarded a half gallon of ice cream for finishing the first half of the Trail.

On this warm July day, I'm standing at a grassy opening near the store ready to ask the first thru-hiker for an interview. Two young men approach me carrying large backpacks.

David and Paul, both 23, are from England and seeing America for the first time by walking the A.T. They seem happy to talk with me – or maybe it's the break from walking. I'm happy to run into them. They're outgoing and friendly and interested in my radio work. I ask if they trained hard for the walk.

"Perhaps we should have, but we didn't really," says David smiling. "Our way of training in England was every Sunday we'd go for a walk without packs, walk a few miles and make sure we hit a pub for a few beers and then walk a few more miles, so it wasn't really in-depth training."

Beginning their walk in Georgia in the spring, they made it to North Carolina before trouble set in.

"We ran into a lot of snow, and that nearly put us off," says David. "If we didn't have 3000 miles to go home, I think we might have been done."

At shelters along the way, journals or "registers" are set out for thru-hikers to write in. Not being a thru-hiker, I've never written in one. But I've stopped on short hikes to read some of the notes.

"It adds a whole new interest to it," says David, "'cause you can put silly comments and jokes in, that sort of thing, tell people behind you that you've passed [them] so hurry up."

Paul and David, sign their notes "The Brits." That's the nickname given to them by fellow hikers. The Brits tell me that America is quite different from what they expected.

"I think the general impression you get in England is it being full of violence the whole time," says David, "'cause all we get is the American detective show on television, that sort of thing. It's not that at all. People have been marvelous."

Two days ago, the Brits walked into the small town of Smithsburg, Mary-Land, as David calls it, to get some mail. When they asked a woman for directions to the post office, she invited them back to her home for breakfast. Then she and her husband cooked up a big American breakfast of bacon, eggs, toast and coffee before taking them to the post office. She made them promise to write when they get home. Right now, they're averaging about seventeen miles of walking a day, but Paul and David think that might change when they get into Maine.

"People say they've been getting within sight of it, Katahdin, the last mountain," says Paul, "as you can see it for 30 miles before you get to it. As soon as you see your final destination, you slow right down, you don't really want to get there – you slow it down to five or six miles a day just to eke it out a bit, a little longer."

David and Paul say they're thinking about taking a bottle of champagne to the summit but that would mean carrying it more than 100 miles from the nearest town. And then, they say, they'd probably drink it long before they get to the top.

For now, they will spend the night at Pine Grove Furnace. There's an old brick building here that serves as a hostel for hikers. It has plenty of beds. At the General Store just down the hill, the two can get sandwiches, sodas and canned food. They'll head out in the morning. I wish them well, these young Englishmen, who instead of visiting Disney World or New York City or some other popular tourist destination, choose to explore America on the Appalachian Trail.

Produced for Public Interest Video Network

TAPE EDITING

Though the need for tape editing has not changed, the technology has. When I first started, radio producers needed to know how to do cut-and-splice editing. It's not something you learn in school but rather on the job. While some networks provided an engineer to work with us, others did not.

When on my own, I dubbed or copied sound bites from my cassette tape onto a reel-to-reel machine where tape moves from one reel to another. Listening to the tape, I'd stop it at the place where I wanted to get rid of unwanted words, sentences or noises. Using a grease pencil, I'd then draw a vertical line on the tape where the edit would begin, then move the tape forward and make another line where the edit would end. Laying that section of tape on a cutting block or bar, I'd cut along the two lines with a sharp razor blade so the unwanted segment would fall out. Joining the ends of the good remaining tape back together in the editing block, I'd place a short piece of splicing tape over the top of the adjoined ends to hold them together with no space in between. I'd always carry a Bandaid in my purse when splice editing tape – just in case I cut my finger with the razor. It only happened once since I learned how to do this from my friend Paul Orsinger, KIX's music director. Paul has a steady hand. He probably never packed a Bandaid.

BASEBALL

It's the beginning of October 1986 and the city of Boston is celebrating. The Red Sox have clinched their division. They'll play a few more regular season games before the playoffs begin. Being a Red Sox fan as far back as I can remember, I'm thinking of ways to cover a game. I convince an editor at The Christian Science Monitor Radio that I know something about baseball, and she gives me the go-ahead to record some interviews with players for a sports show.

This warm fall evening I'm headed to Fenway Park – home of the Red Sox. The Baltimore Orioles are in town with Manager Earl Weaver coaching one of his last games. He recently announced his retirement at the end of the season.

Dennis "Oil Can" Boyd, a flamboyant, talkative player for the Sox will get the start tonight. On arriving at the Park, I see him already on the field surrounded by reporters. I'm taking the whole scene in – the field, the stands, Fenway's famous left field wall known as the Green Monster – when Red Sox pitcher Tom Seaver walks by quickly towards the dugout. He doesn't look interested in talking to any reporters. Third baseman Wade Boggs passes by, smiles and winks – or is that a fleck of dirt in his eye? I spot Spike Owen, the 25-year old shortstop who was traded to the Red Sox during the season from Seattle. I approach him, introduce myself and ask if we can talk. He's agreeable. As we sit down in the dugout, it begins to feel surreal – apparently for both of us. Spike says he can't believe he's here – never expected to be getting ready for the playoffs. When a photographer, who's standing outside the dugout, snaps a picture of Spike and me, I want to run onto the field and give the man my name and address so he can send me a copy. I don't do it, thinking it'll look stupid, but I wish I had!

Relief pitcher Bob Stanley is nearby and looks interested in talking with me. I learn later that Stanley has made more career appearances for the Red Sox than any other pitcher in team history. Stanley is tall – 6 feet 4 inches and heavy set. His teammates have nicknamed him the "Steamer" after the "Stanley Steamer" – a steam powered automobile of the early 1900's famous for its world speed record, and which now is extremely rare. There's a gentleness about Stanley. He's soft spoken and matter of fact.

"How's the pitching?" I ask, unsure of how his season is going.

"In any job you have good days, you have bad days. That's the way it's been so far."

It's well known that pitchers fear Fenway Park's Green Monster. The wall rises up in shallow left field making it most enticing for home run hitters.

"What's it like pitching in Fenway?" I ask.

"It's a tough day when the wind's blowing out. It's a good day when the wind's blowing in, so you have a 50/50 chance of having a good day. You have to make good pitches here – keep the ball down."

Stanley's specialty is the sinker ball which sinks rapidly when reaching the plate. He relies on getting a lot of double play grounders from it.

"How do you feel about going into the World Series?"

"We're not there yet. We still have to go to the playoffs and that's just as important. You get nervous, and you try to do the best you can," says the calm man next to me who will soon be in the center of the storm.

Looking over at the visiting team's dugout, I see that Earl Weaver is all smiles watching the excitement around him. Thinking back, I wish I'd interviewed Earl and sold some of the sound bites to Baltimore and Washington stations. I'd have made more money. Better yet, I'd have talked with one of the greatest managers in the history of the game! But at the time I was focused solely on the Red Sox.

I end up interviewing several Red Sox players after the game. In the locker room I find Jim Rice, the Sox's power-hitting left fielder, who's destined one day for Baseball's Hall of Fame.

In the last year, I've picked up the habit of saying to everyone I interview: "Could you tell me your name for a voice test?" As they say their name I adjust the level on my recorder.

"Let's get a sound test … just give me your name," I say to Jim.

"If you don't know my name, sweetheart, I'm not telling you," he replies.

It's not a response I'm expecting and I don't say anything.

But Jim Rice turns out to be easy to talk with and a good interview. He tells me that in the remaining regular season games, "starters" should be played – that they should be on the field for at least six innings. There's no way Jim Rice wants to sit and watch and rest. Behind Jim as he's talking, right fielder Dwight Evans puts gear into his locker. For years I've watched Evans and Rice play baseball on TV. It's incredible to see them now in this setting.

I flash back to when I wanted to be a sportscaster. The thought hasn't lost its appeal. I need to do more with sports!

Postscript

The Red Sox win the playoffs and advance to the World Series against the New York Mets. With a 3-2 lead in the World Series, they enter Game 6, which goes extra innings. In the bottom of the 10th inning with two outs and Mets player Mookie Wilson at bat, Bob Stanley, The Steamer, throws a wild pitch bringing in a runner from third base to tie the game. The Mets go on to win the game and the next one, too, to clinch the World Series.

I think about how Bob Stanley must have felt, the pressure that he and other relievers face in their job and how they deal with it. It can't be easy. I once heard a pitcher-turned-sportscaster (whose name I've forgotten) say that when a reliever loses a game, he needs to blot it out before going into the next one. Stanley will have a long off-season to try and blot out this one.

NARRATION

What else can I do with this job? While I'm narrating my own feature stories, I'm also looking for opportunities to "voice" public service announcements (PSA's), television documentaries and commercials. Narrations pay well and can be very lucrative with TV network programs. Using my audition tape from KIX, I land several narration jobs from a small production company in downtown Washington. Two of the scripts are PSA's for Ralph Nader's consumer advocacy groups. I'm glad to do narrations for Nader, who spoke to my graduating class at Connecticut College in the early 1970's. Nader is from the northwestern Connecticut town of Winsted, not far from where I grew up. An old mill town at the convergence of two rivers, Winsted was devastated by hurricanes and flooding in 1955. The mills are gone with some of the buildings renovated into office space. Years from now Nader will build an unusual museum in Winsted – one that's about tort law.

A group called North American Network (NAN) hires me to narrate some PSA's and to record some speeches including a couple at the National Press Club in downtown Washington. The recording ('hook-up') is pretty simple work. Reporters just plug their recorders into a large black box before the speech begins and unplug at the end. I take the recording back to NAN headquarters. The job earns me $75.

Sometimes freelancers, who are not regular hired staff in an organization, have trouble getting paid. As my workload for NAN increases, I notice a disturbing trend. NAN has a problem with paying me on time. A couple months often goes by with no check so I call to inquire. I forget the excuses given, but it's never that the check is in the mail. One day when calling, I reach an older unfamiliar voice. After explaining to him my frustration at having to continually badger them about paychecks, there's a pause. I wonder what he'll say? He apologizes and promises to fix the problem immediately. And he does. The next day a check arrives in the mail.

"Who was that guy?" I wonder. I still don't know, but from then on, I never have to make a complaint call again.

What I like best about working with NAN is their annual summer employee picnic, which I'm invited to attend. It's fun and a good way to meet people and drum up some business. Most of the time I don't know anyone at the event, except a couple of people I've talked to on the phone (not the ones who've listened to my complaints). But I always leave the picnic with names and phone numbers and hopes for future work. Looking for narration work is never-ending, the same goes for finding ideas and cranking out feature stories!

SCUFFY DUCK

"What's happening?" was a favorite greeting in my high school days. Well, at a minor-league baseball game one summer afternoon in Hagerstown, Maryland, "Scuffy Duck" is what's happening. Scuffy is the mascot for the Hagerstown Suns, the Single A farm team of the Baltimore Orioles. As just another baseball fan, I'm watching him from the stands in his orange and black duck suit. Scuffy is all over the field break-dancing, skateboarding, somersaulting. He's the star of the show. Forget about the game. Kids in the stands are screaming and laughing – so are their parents. I'm thinking: here's a good summer feature story! So, I call Monitor Radio and get approval for a show.

Jeremy Bingaman (aka Scuffy), who's sixteen and a junior in high school, officially works for a local radio station, WYII, where he takes calls and answers fan mail. I meet him before a day game when he's not yet in mascot uniform.

"Why do the kids like you so much?" I ask him.

He smiles.

"I can get by with things they would like to get by with. I guess it's like a live cartoon character. They just think it's cool."

But in fact, it's hot, really hot inside the duck suit on summer days. However, Jeremy says he'd rather be in it than out.

"I couldn't go out there without the suit – with people knowing who I was, because I don't like to make a fool of myself," he explains, laughing.

I'm wondering what this young man will be doing in ten or twenty years. He's smart, energetic, funny and likes people. And he works hard. He hands me his baseball card. It's a good picture of him. He's got his serious duck face on. His idol, he tells me, is the Chicken, the part-time mascot of the major league San Diego Padres.

"You're kidding?" I'm amazed.

Years ago, when living in southern California, I took in a few Padre games with my brother. We laughed ourselves silly watching the Chicken mimic everyone – players, coaches, umpires, fans. Jeremy says he envies the Chicken because he has props. Jeremy's favorite is the one of the umpire, which gets kicked around a lot. If he could afford props, Jeremy says that he'd be doing something different and funny every day in his routine.

Not that he needs to. Later that afternoon during the game, he's up in the bleachers with kids lined up waiting for an autograph or a hug. No one's paying any attention to the players. It's Scuffy Duck that's happening!

BERNIE

I get the shocking news that Bernie Adams has died. It was a brain aneurysm or something like it – one minute, Bernie is here, the next he is gone. I am devastated as is everyone I know who knows him. Sandy Zimmet and I go to the service in Frederick. Luckily, Sandy brings a box of Kleenex as the two of us weep throughout.

As I listen to people speak, my mind wanders back to the last time I saw Bernie. We had met for lunch at a restaurant in Frederick. He wanted to hear all about what I'd been doing in radio. As we ate and talked, many folks came over to our table to say hello to him. They seemed excited to see him. I think it was then I realized what Bernie meant to this community, how much he was liked and respected. I'd gotten a sense of it at WFMD when putting my documentary together. Whenever I called people for interviews and I mentioned his name, they immediately agreed to meet me. I knew they trusted him, which is so vital in radio.

I think I took it for granted – the trust he had in me. There was that time when I gave him the script of my documentary (six pages) for him to read and edit. I expected changes to what I'd written, for he was the expert and I the novice. He read each page carefully then handed it back to me – without changing a word. Right afterwards, we produced the documentary with Bernie at the console controlling the taping and me narrating. I'll never forget my excitement.

Looking up at the lectern, Bernie's reporter, Randy Gray, is getting ready to speak. But as he does his eyes fill with tears, and he chokes up. This is the saddest day I can ever remember.

THE STORY OF ECHO HILL

Sipping a cup of coffee one morning and browsing through the Washington Post classifieds, I notice an interesting Help Wanted ad. An environmental adventure school on the Chesapeake Bay called Echo Hill Outdoor School is looking for teachers. While I've never done an environmental education story featuring kids, I'd like to try. Interviewing kids is usually fun and interesting, maybe because I rarely have a clue what they're going to say. I telephone Echo Hill and learn that a school director, Andrew McCown, can take me out on the Bay in Echo Hill's fishing boat along with a group of kids visiting from a middle school in Philadelphia.

On a warm fall day, I head for the Eastern Shore of Maryland and drive across the Chesapeake Bay Bridge. Way up high on the bridge, I take in the view up and down the Chesapeake. If I'd known then where to look, I would have known I could almost see Echo Hill from there. It's on the eastern shore of the Bay (always written: Eastern Shore) and north of the bridge. In forty-five minutes, I cross the Chester River into historic Chestertown, Maryland. The road, lined with large maple and oak trees, leads past the campus of Washington College with its Georgian style red brick buildings and expansive green lawns. I make a mental note to return to this beautiful place for a visit.

In another half-hour, I'll head up the long, sandy road to Echo Hill and find Andrew McCown, better known as "Captain Andy." He's easy to spot with all the excited seventh graders in tow. The kids are putting on their life jackets as they climb aboard Echo Hill's 44-foot fishing boat for a class called "Chesapeake Bay Studies."

Before starting up the engine, Andrew McCown recites the rules.

"Rule Number 1 – no swimming. You cannot fall off the boat – it's against the rules," he says to the kids circled around him. "Rule Number 2 – keep life jackets on. Rule 3 – Feet in the boat. Rule 4 – You need to have fun. It's against the rules not to have fun!"

A cheer goes up, and Captain Andy starts the engine. There's excitement on a lot of young faces as we motor out from the pier. Captain Andy starts talking about estuaries and plankton and food chains.

"What age did the estuary grow out of?" asks the Captain.

"Ice," one boy yells.

"Yeah."

Out on the Bay the kids pull up a crab pot with a large crab hanging off the side. When a girl screams, I've got it on tape. There are lots of sounds out here on the water – some of them will be dropped into the program later on in the studio during production.

The boat speeds up and cuts through the water. The wind feels good in my face. I can taste a little salt. Then Andy slows the boat. The kids gather around as he leaves the helm to haul up a net with some fish in it. He pulls one out.

"This is a rockfish, striped bass. This guy, he gets to be 80 to 100 pounds, six to seven feet long. What does he eat, do you think?"

"Plankton?" says one youngster.

"No, he's not a plankton eater."

"Little fish," another child pipes in.

"Little fish," agrees the Captain. "Suppose he's this long?" He moves his fingers apart. "He'd eat crab. There was a time in the 1920's when watermen caught so many of them they were actually a trash fish and were given or sold to farmers to use as fertilizer."

Everything that's taken out of the water goes back in, says McCown, although, a few fish live on the boat. They're swimming around inside a small aquarium that the kids continually walk by and peer into. All the fish are native to the Chesapeake. Captain Andy takes a tiny net, dips it into the aquarium and scoops out a shiny white fish with a black dot near its gill.

"This is a spot," he says.

The kids move in for a closer look. As the boat bobs in the water, a flock of seagulls screeches overhead. They can barely be heard above the commotion below.

I ask a boy what he thinks about this floating classroom.

"You're learning about the outside life," he says, "learning to appreciate things more than just lay on a couch and watch TV. We're talking about nature and wildlife."

Produced for Mutual Broadcasting System

DINOSAUR MUSEUM

I'll never forget interviewing my daughter, Lucy, for a feature story. She was three years old at the time, and we were in Montana.

It happens in the Museum of the Rockies, a part of Montana State University in Bozeman, which is well-known for its dinosaur research. Excavations in Montana of dino eggs, bones and skeletons have altered some dinosaur theories. Mutual News is interested in a two-minute science piece about the developments. So, when my husband, Buzz, has a business conference in Red Lodge, Montana, I buy a ticket for Lucy and me to go along. Our first stop is the Museum of the Rockies.

The Museum's Director of Education, David Swingle, tells us that millions of years ago a volcano near here killed a herd of ten thousand dinosaurs along with other reptiles and amphibians and insects. In the long-standing debate over whether dinosaurs were warm blooded or coldblooded, Swingle says they were probably warm blooded – and fairly intelligent, and that some species took care of their young.

Near us, a herd of real-looking dinosaurs is attracting a crowd. The dinos – part of a robotic exhibit from Japan – are moving! One of them looks terrified standing over a helpless-looking baby as a group of predatory dinosaurs and huge lizards stalk the nest. The creatures are making eerie sounds.

Lucy is taking it all in while trying to climb up into her father's arms. My recorder is already on when I ask what she thinks. Lucy's never at a loss for words.

"Those dinosaurs are scary. They look like they were alive a long time ago," she says, clinging to her dad.

Now, that's enough of this dinosaur exhibit; she wants to move on to the Planetarium.

Back home when putting my radio story together, I decide to use some sound bites of people seeing the exhibit. While I may be a little biased here – I think it's the sound of the three-year old who steals the show!

CANDIDATE BILL CLINTON

In politics, it's sometimes the crowd that makes the story. In early 1992 Pacifica Network hires me to cover a Maryland Democratic primary event in Baltimore. Former Arkansas Governor Bill Clinton is speaking at a black church downtown. Clinton is running against former Senator Paul Tsongas of Massachusetts and Governor Jerry Brown of California. At this stage in the primaries, he is not the frontrunner. He has lost the Iowa Caucuses to Iowa Senator Tom Harkin and the New Hampshire primary to Tsongas. But he's working had to promote a comeback.

Hundreds of black men and women fill the church. Black leaders like Baltimore Mayor, Kurt Schmoke, are in attendance.

Clinton is getting laryngitis. His speech is strained and long and filled with promises – many of them greeted with cheers and applause.

"You'll never have to worry whether I get up every day and go to bat and try to get a hit and make some progress on the common problems of the country," he says. "I got into politics because I could not stand the thought of people growing up and not living up to their God-given potential – and I'm running for President because that is not happening today, and I can do better."

After the speech Clinton joins the crowd gathered outside the church. He is nearly smothered by people trying to get close to him. Only two reporters are here to record the moment and see Bill Clinton press the flesh – a reporter from NPR, and me. It is as though Clinton is in a wave. When he moves, a mass of people move with him. He never stops talking – seemingly to everyone around him. But when answering a question or signing an autograph, he makes eye contact with that one person. Clinton's magnetism is something to behold – but about to be interrupted. A bodyguard moves between the candidate and his following, guiding Clinton to a car that takes him away.

My husband asks me that night what I think about the Presidential race. I tell him that Bill Clinton will be our next President.

FISHING AND HUNTING (Sort of)

I love to fish. I learned to fly fish watching my father on our dock on Doolittle Lake in Connecticut. My father could cast a fly as far as the eye could see and land it lightly on the water. He'd know just where a trout was feeding. He'd see it make a swirl as it ate a bug, then cast his fly close to the swirl. The cruising fish often came back for a look at the new fly and would grab it. My casts looked like I was skipping a stone on the water – short and splashy. I didn't fool many fish, but I practiced and got better.

Producing the catch and release story for radio all these years later was exciting. I'm hoping to do more fishing stories when I read about a sport called bow fishing in a Pennsylvania magazine. Bow fishing is different from anything I've ever experienced, but it sounds interesting.

Fishermen use a bow and special arrows that have fishing line attached to shoot at giant carp in rivers. Trophy carp can weigh 50 pounds. This story, as far as I know, has never been done for radio. Perfect.

Codorus Creek runs along the east side of York, Pennsylvania (self-proclaimed Factory Capital of the World and home of the Harley Davidson motorcycle). At the river access off Black Rock Road I meet Jeff and Jason, two young men who've agreed to take me bow fishing. They are already putting on their waders – chest-high with shoulder straps. Looking at my much shorter hip boots, it crosses my mind that I might be in for some trouble. As we wade out into the stream, the water inches up to nearly the top of my boots. Any higher and I'll be underwater – equipment and all. Holding my tape recorder and microphone up next to my head, as far from the splashing water as I can, I feel something strange around my feet. Jeff knows what it is right away.

"Those holes you're stepping in are carp nests. They're spawning. You can just watch the trail where they're going."

"Wow!"

I wonder what stepping in those holes without boots on would feel like.

Wading upstream into shallow water, Jeff spots a fish under a tree hanging out over the creek. We stop about fifteen feet away. He raises his bow, takes aim and shoots. As the arrow whizzes by, I'm taping. But it misses the target, and the fish takes off with a splash. Jeff winds the line back in onto a reel mounted on the inside of his bow. Like all fishing, bow fishing takes patience.

We keep moving as quietly as we can so as not to spook any fish.

"Look, there's a little bass." Jeff points at a fish close by. But it's not one he's interested in catching today.

It feels good being out on the water in the warm sunshine, but Jeff and Jason get off only a couple more shots. No luck. We head back in empty-handed, talking about trying it again sometime.

My editor at NPR doesn't seem at all disappointed to learn that no carp are caught. As is often the case with fishing, the fish are victorious. That's why they call it 'fishing' and not 'catching.'

SAW MUSICIAN

I really enjoy finding off-beat radio stories that no one has done before. While reading Pennsylvania Magazine, I come across a short article about a woman who plays the saw as a musical instrument. Here's something new and different! It takes only a couple minutes of talking with musician Janice Vieldhouse on the telephone to know she'll be a good interview for a show. She's interesting and friendly. After getting directions to her home in Chester County, about 30 miles northwest of Philadelphia, I begin my latest adventure.

Janice wants to be interviewed while sitting in her kitchen. While some people hang pots and pans from their kitchen ceiling, Janice hangs her collection of saws. There's one right over my head, and it looks quite sharp. I scoot my chair over to avoid a direct hit.

Janice tells me she has played the saw for years — ever since her husband's grandmother sent her a saw in the mail as a wedding gift. The grandmother was a legendary sawyer and once played with Liberace.

Janice shows me how she does it. She plays sitting down, holding the saw upright between her knees. With her left-hand atop the end of the saw she bends the blade back and forth in an S-shape while moving a cello bow across the saw's smooth side. How much she bends the blade, and where on the saw she draws the bow determines the notes. She demonstrates by playing "Edelweiss." Her saw seems to sing in a soprano pitch. It's a little spooky, like nothing I've ever heard.

"You know you can throw it around," she says, and throws the saw onto the floor. "It doesn't hurt it at all."

I burst out laughing. Didn't see that coming. This interview is getting fun, and Janice is just getting going.

"Have you seen my chainsaw?"

"You play a chainsaw?"

"I haven't been practicing up on it, but this man made me this saw with two holes in the blade and a chain hanging down. There's a piston on top with a wire going down."

"So, you can play it?"

"Well, the chain rattles a lot so it's not too nice."

"You play all these saws?" I'm looking up at the ceiling.

Janice nods. "It's fun to play and see peoples' faces and then let them try it. A lot of people want lessons."

Vieldhouse, who also plays drums, performs at variety shows, music festivals and parties for friends. When I leave she gives me a cassette of her songs, which includes "America the Beautiful" and Elvis Presley's "Hound Dog" among others. I'll use the music in three different shows that I produce for three networks – Voice of America, The Christian Science Monitor Radio, and Mutual Broadcasting. The producer at Mutual is disappointed that I don't have any sound of Janice playing her chainsaw. Now why didn't I think of that?

BOBSLEDDING

Lake Placid, New York is a beautiful place. I'm here to do a story on the U.S. National Bobsled Team competing in the World Cup. The team is staying at the Mirror Lake Inn. Walking in the front door with equipment bag in hand, I notice a group of athletes milling around the lobby. Not knowing anyone but having the name of one team member, I approach a friendly looking fellow in the crowd and ask, "Do you know Brian Shimer?"

"I'm Brian Shimer," he says.

I'm off to a good start!

Finding a quiet guest room away from the noise in the lobby, we sit down to talk. Shimer (pronounced Shymer) is from Naples, Florida. He was a high school wrestling champion, then went on to college where he played football and ran track. He says he'd never been in a bobsled before being chosen for the U.S. team, but won a spot by passing a fitness test made up of sprints, shot put, long jump and high jump.

"Bobsledders need to be fast and strong," says my next interview, team coach John Morgan. "Speed and strength are crucial in pushing a sled across slippery ice at the start of the bobsled race."

For about 45 yards, bobsledders charge down the ice pushing the sled before jumping in it. While the race takes about a minute to run, I'm told that bobsledders spend the next three to four hours repairing the sled from the beating it's taken. They wax it, polish and sand the runners or blades until the scratches are out. They tighten nuts and bolts and check for any cracks. A lot goes into making it as safe and fast as it can be.

Walking the trail that runs alongside the one-mile bobsled track, sleds speed by me in stretches at nearly 100 miles an hour. I'm thinking about what bobsledder Jeff Hayes told me – that the sport isn't for everyone.

"If you like riding rollercoasters and you like driving fast," says Hayes, "I guess it's the sport for you."

Since I like both, maybe it is. It's sure fun to watch. The speeding sleds make good background sound for my story. I also tape the voice on the loud speaker announcing races. I'm cold standing out next to the track but luckily brought along gloves that keep my hands from freezing to my metal microphone.

On my way back to Washington, I retrace my route – an easy drive to the ferry crossing and scenic ride across Lake Champlain to Burlington where I drop off my rental car and board a plane to National Airport (now Reagan National).

With all the expenses involved in travel, I make no money on this show but have now produced another program for NPR's "Morning Edition," seen Lake Placid and learned something about bobsledding. And as my husband said encouragingly the morning of my planned trip when I hesitated about going, "What else do you have going on today?"

BE THERE

Showing up may well be the most important part of freelancing. (See Bobsledding story, for example.) Most of the time, I need to get to a place I've never been to before, one that's not nearby. Often, it's on a weekend. I need to be there early – well before the scheduled interview(s) to tape two or three minutes of the sounds of the place to use later on in my show, and to scout out any potential problems like excess noise, which I want to avoid during taping. While this isn't the most exciting part of feature work, it's essential.

The exciting part is finding the story idea, pitching it to editors in a way they can't resist, interviewing, writing and narrating. All of these things produce an endorphin-like high. It's intoxicating. After the story airs, there's a let-down. But, then there's another idea that turns into another show that reaches millions of people and tells them something new and interesting.

Of course, it doesn't always work this way. Some story ideas don't get approved; they may already have been used, or don't pique the interest of editors. Sometimes shows that are all set to air don't because of unforeseen news events that supersede regular programming. It's all part of the work. But the work goes on…and on.

JIM DICKSON

It would take a lot of courage to sail alone across the Atlantic Ocean. But to be blind and attempt it is beyond anything I can comprehend. So begins my interest in Jim Dickson. Dickson, who is 41, has been blind since childhood. He taught himself to sail and also loves to ski. I read about his planned ocean crossing aboard a 36-foot sailboat named *Eye-Opener* and phone him to see if he'll talk with me about it. He invites me to meet him in Washington DC.

There is a lot I want to ask Dickson — especially: "How will you do this?" In the next half-hour, he explains. He knows where everything is located on the boat — where the lines are and all the equipment. And just the feel of the boat — the way it heels and rides over the waves, the sounds of the wind in the rigging — tells him a lot about wind and sea conditions. He'll use a voice synthesized computer. A program that fits in the PC hooks up to marine navigation equipment that he says enables a blind person to hear what a sighted person would see on a screen — wind speed, compass heading, boat position. For backup, in case of equipment failure, he'll use a braille compass. It seems like he's thought of everything. Since he'll be harnessed to the boat, which is common for sailors crossing the ocean, there's no chance, he says, of falling off. Or at least falling off and still not being attached! He'll have radio contact with someone on shore. His position will be tracked; people will know where he is at all times in case of an emergency. He has a lot of help in this effort, for sure, and sounds very confident.

"I'll have one hell of a good time," says Dickson, but adds he expects a mixture of boredom, exhilaration and terror. He convinces me, sort of, that everything will be alright.

The more Jim talks about his upcoming 2500-mile voyage, the more I hear a recurring theme — that blind people can do things that others don't expect them to do. Too many blind people in America can't find jobs when the technology is there, he tells me. Blind people can work in all kinds of employment settings that may not have been possible before. It occurs to me that Jim Dickson is not just making this trip for himself but for many others like him.

Postscript

I read later that Dickson's voyage ended before he reached Europe. He was forced to stop. I don't recall whether it was because of a storm or equipment failure or something else. But it is his bravery in embarking on the journey that lives on in my memory.

Produced for The Christian Science Monitor Radio

LAKE WALES RIDGE

An article and photograph in an obscure magazine called "Garbage" grabs my attention. It's about an area in central Florida called Lake Wales Ridge. Millions of years ago the ocean covered all of Florida except this long sandy ridge about 10 miles wide and 100 miles long that stretches down the center of the state. On this ancient sand dune is one of the largest concentrations of rare plants in the world.

During a vacation in Florida I take a day and drive inland towards Lake Wales Ridge past cattle ranches and horse farms – a vastly different landscape from the endless strip malls and housing developments near Florida's coast.

I meet up with John Fitzpatrick, who heads the Archbold Biological Station, a research, conservation and education center in the midst of this land known as scrub. He puts a pair of binoculars around his neck, and we set out on a walk through deep sugary sand that is covered with stunted oak trees, cactus and scraggly bushes. There is a stark beauty here on Lake Wales Ridge where we're standing about 130 feet above sea level. (In spots, it's as high as 200 feet above sea level).

Fitzpatrick calls to the birds, specifically the threatened Florida scrub jay. He hands me a peanut and tells me to hold it out between my thumb and finger. Sure enough, a foot-long blue and gray bird flies in and begins pecking at my peanut.

"Ouch!"

Feels like the scrub jay may be getting a little bit of my finger along with the nut. Fitzpatrick isn't feeling any pain. He feeds the jays from both hands. One jay has landed on his head. He's named them all and knows which are the parents and which the offspring. I'm thinking that my grandfather should be here. He loved birds. He used to whistle to them, and they'd whistle back.

"Do they know you or recognize you?" I ask Fitzpatrick.

He smiles.

"It's possible they recognize most frequent visitors, but in fact they treat any human with a peanut as a pretty good friend."

Peanuts are like tasty acorns, which is a major food source here for scrub jays. They get acorns from the scrub oaks.

"Now you take a bulldozer to that scrub where they've buried their acorns for the fall," says Fitzpatrick, "they can't move elsewhere, can't do anything else – other scrub is occupied, acorns are gone. So, what happens? They die a slow starving death looking for shelter and places they don't know. The common myth that you take the habitat away and they go somewhere else is just false. These things have evolved here – have been here a million years."

It is a passionate plea for saving Lake Wales Ridge – one that Fitzpatrick will soon see answered. The following year (1993) Congress designates a portion of Lake Wales Ridge as a National Wildlife Refuge to protect rare plants – the first of its kind in the country.

Postscript

Not only am I fascinated with what I learn from this story, but the story is also a way for me to let many others know about these kinds of conservation efforts – or in the case of Jim Dickson, get people thinking about those who take on extraordinary challenges. The story helps not only me, but others as well.

Produced for Mutual Broadcasting System

CIRCUS SMIRKUS

Friends and family know what I do and often offer their ideas. My niece gives me a story idea while I'm on summer vacation in Maine. A friend of hers, who wants to join the circus, is at a circus camp in New Hampshire. It's about a three-hour drive away, but I'm thinking it will be time well spent. With all the excitement surrounding kids and the circus, this will make a fun summer feature story. As often occurs in the summer, networks are looking for more freelance stories since so many of their fulltime correspondents are on vacation. And this proves to be the case when Mutual Broadcasting shows interest in the piece.

The camp takes place on a hill in the White Mountains not far from a small town called Bethlehem. When driving up to the hilltop, I pull over to the side of the road and look at the spectacular view of surrounding mountain ranges. It inspires another mental note to return to this place some day when I'm not working.

Walking through the door into Circus Smirkus Camp is like walking into the Big Top – but all the performers are kids. They're riding by on unicycles, walking on stilts, juggling and tumbling. Having been in the car for hours, I'm thinking here's my chance to get some exercise chasing them around.

Camp Director Mary Blouin, who meets me near the door, confirms what I'm already noticing – that skill, physical strength and coordination play a big role in circus arts. She introduces me to some of the kids, who seem more than happy to talk with me.

One ten-year old boy has made 260 jumps on a pogo stick. He counted.

"What kinds of things are you learning? I ask.

"How to juggle clubs, how to juggle period, perch – which is the long metal pole – trapeze and climbing," he says, smiling ear to ear.

A nine-year old is on what's called a rolling globe.

"Is it hard to do?" I inquire.

"It's pretty hard if you don't know how to do it," he says. "All you have to do is move your feet from side to side to keep it from tipping over and throwing you off."

Another child chimes in. "Once you learn how to juggle, it's pretty easy to do it on the rolling globe."

Seriously?

"Want to try it?" asks the nine-year old.

"Um, better not today," I say, picturing myself lying flat on my face.

Nearby a girl is juggling scarves.

"They're easier than balls because they come down slower, so you have time to catch them. It's better for beginners. It's really fun," she says.

"And that's not all," adds the camper friend beside her. "You get to do a lot of stuff your parents yell at you for. Like, don't juggle plates, don't take our scarves and try to juggle them, and don't stand on that bowl and try to walk on it!"

The kids are engaged and excited. Some of them will join Circus Smirkus, a children's circus tour in New England. Others say that it's fun just telling their friends they've been to circus camp and seeing the expressions on their friends' faces.

Produced for Mutual Broadcasting

LOS EBANOS

The once mighty Rio Grande River is running out of water, drained nearly dry in some areas from dams for irrigation, hydroelectric power and reservoirs. In southeastern Texas I begin work on a half hour documentary for Voice of America about the river's predicament. In the course of gathering interviews for the show, I come across a fascinating piece of history. The little village of Los Ebanos, named for its many ebony trees, sits alongside the Rio Grande River, which runs between the borders of Mexico and the U.S. It is said that Spanish explorers crossed the Rio Grande here, as did Texas Rangers chasing cattle rustlers, and smugglers escaping Prohibition. Steep-cut banks as high as 15-feet and a line of trees along the bank mark this ancient ford.

In 1950 a ferry and inspection station were set up at Los Ebanos. It is the only government licensed hand-pulled ferry on a U.S. border. By pulling on a cable that spans this narrow stretch of river, five men drag the boat from one side of the Rio Grande to the other. Just three cars and a few walk-on passengers fit aboard. Passengers, I'm told, have been known to grab hold of the rope and help workers pull the ferry across. I also learn that most of the people going back and forth across the river here are from the town of Diaz Ordaz in the Tamaulipas state of Mexico.

It is an odd feeling looking across the river into another country that appears no different from mine. I wonder what life is like for those who live there.

I ask permission from the ferry manager to tape interviews for a short feature. When he consents I board the boat, radio equipment in hand. Four women come aboard behind me and smile. Pulling off from the landing, I approach two of the workmen whose hands are in thick gloves and are gripping the cable.

"What's it like, heavy?" I ask.

When they say something back to me, it's not in words I can understand.

As I make my way around the boat I find that no one speaks any English. Unfortunately for me, I don't speak any Spanish. While the young women and I try using simple words in our own language, it's no help. I even try speaking some French (my French being a little better than my Spanish). Nothing works. My idea of a short, last-minute story fails, yet it is still an amazing experience for me. For here I am, riding across an historic, dramatic and beautiful part of one of the most famous rivers in America.

NARRATION CONTINUED

With some help from a friend whose husband is on the Board of Directors of Discovery Channel, I get my resume and audition tape passed on to a producer at Discovery. My hope is to land an audition for a show. I'm really excited when the network just assigns me a show to narrate. It's a one-hour TV program for "Wild Discovery" about Colobus monkeys. The script arrives and a date is set for taping in the network's studio near Arlington, Virginia.

No time is a good time to get a cold but this is a really bad time. For ten days before the scheduled taping, I'm fighting one. The taping has to be postponed. In an office visit with my doctor the day before my second and presumably last chance at taping, I tell him that I'm on the verge of losing a big job opportunity and please can he find a way for me to sound better by tomorrow. Keep doing what you're doing, he says. I'm gargling warm salted water, breathing over a steaming tea kettle and taking medication. Miraculously, I wake up the next day with my head and sinuses clear.

Arriving at Discovery's studio, I meet the show's producer who's polite and friendly. He hands me a 26-page final copy of the script and escorts me to a small recording booth. Then he joins an engineer in the Control Room. Peering through a glass window between us, I see that he looks very serious – nervous, maybe. I'm thinking that he has no idea how I'll do with this narration. Since there was no audition, he has never heard me read before. For all he knows, I could be terrible. The engineer asks me to read a couple lines for a level on my voice. We're ready to start.

As always with narrations, I take a deep breath, then begin. I'm through the first few pages with no stumbles and only a few re-takes. The script reads easily, which is not always the case – but today it flows. I'm enjoying reading about a family of Colobus monkeys in West Africa – the youngest named Pip, his older brother, Punk, and their mother Prune.

When we take a short break and the producer steps out of the studio, I can see he's smiling. Is it the script - or maybe he's thinking the narration won't be as bad as he expected? I don't stop him to ask.

A couple months later Discovery sends me another script. This one is about butterflies. Thinking this read will be as easy as my last, I'm in for a big surprise.

Sitting in the same booth, I'm looking again through the glass window at the engineer and producer and awaiting instructions, but this time when I start to read and get into the rhythm of the script, the producer interrupts, then interrupts again asking me to correct a mistake that I'm continually making. For example, when reading: "The butterfly has migrated…" I emphasize "butterfly" and pause a split second between "butterfly" and "has." The producer wants that part of the sentence to come together without any pause or emphasis. It's a small difference, but it's what he wants. Also, I'm ending every sentence the same way by dropping my voice. I need to end sentences on an up-note from time to time to avoid being boring.

Narrating is a lot harder than it sounds. It takes lots of reading practice to sound natural with the right pace. Where you put emphasis in a sentence, and even in a single word, how you pitch your voice, depending upon what the narration is describing, when and how you breathe – all are part of doing the kind of professional job each producer is looking for. Bernie Adams told me early on in my internship to read newspapers out loud for narration practice, so I do that a lot.

In this narration, I finally get into the rhythm and finish it up.

A RADIO FAMILY

Freelancers aren't bona-fide members of any radio family. They aren't around enough to become familiar faces. But at Voice of America I'm starting to feel at home when going in to produce my stories. VOA, which airs programs around the world but not in the U.S., has its headquarters on the National Mall in Washington, about a block away from the Air and Space Museum. Over the years I've worked with several editors and engineers at Voice of America, but these days I'm working mostly with engineer, Bob Doughty, who loves to laugh and joke and who always produces shows that are technically perfect, and with editor, Faith Lapidus. Faith is VOA's editor for freelance producers. Like Bob, she's fun to work with. I'm finding that most people I deal with in radio have a good sense of humor. If they didn't, I might well be doing something else. "If the job's no fun, what's the point?" as my friend Hilda would say.

Editing and narrating are demanding and a big part of feature work. In working with Faith on edits, I always know what to expect. There's a routine we follow. After emailing her my script with suggested sound bites, she edits sentences to make them read better; she double-checks all the facts, and sometimes asks for more of them. She may ask me to move a sound bite or include another one. Once in a while she tells me that I need to do another interview to add another voice to the show. That means a lot more work needs to be done. But the story improves with edits. With any major ones, she always asks if I'm comfortable with it. If I'm not, they're not made.

By the time I show up at VOA's headquarters to produce my show, I've been through several edits, and have finished the editing stage. It's time to mix the show – to combine sound bites and background sound (ambience) with my narration of the script.

In the production studio, engineer Bob Doughty and I transfer sound bites from my cassette to his computer. Then he digitally edits them, trimming off dead sound or unwanted noises like a cough or slamming door. It's fun watching him edit sound digitally. Digital isn't a word I use much except when I tell people I'm digitally challenged. I'm still using the tape recorder I bought 30 years ago. It has great quality and my editors accept it, although Bob keeps encouraging me to go digital.

Since I've already rehearsed reading the copy in my office at home, I'm ready to voice the show. I take a seat in the recording studio. These days, more often than not, I don't put on the headphones because hearing my voice through them makes my voice sound better – more resonant – than it really is. Without headphones, I hear my real voice – the one being taped and the one I need to be working with for the best results.

Hanging down in front of me in the studio is a microphone which might need a small adjustment so it's close to my mouth and slightly to one side. As I read a line or two of my script, Bob, who's looking at me through a glass window and listening to me read, makes adjustments on the console. He gets a good level on my voice. Then he gives me a hand cue and I begin reading. When I come to a break in the copy for a sound bite, I stop reading and Bob drops the sound bite in. As it ends he gives me another cue and I pick up where I left off. At intervals Bob mixes in some of the background sound that I gathered at the scene of the story and which now helps put the listener there.

Hearing the piece come together is exciting. A lot of work has gone into interviewing, writing and editing. The way it plays out now makes it seem easy.

CONTACTS

My address book is filling up with names. Covering three pages are the names and phone numbers of twenty-six people at The Christian Science Monitor Radio. Names include editors and producers for the daily show and the weekend show, an archivist to help with research questions, a person in the payments department who has information on expense accounting. Most everyone at Monitor works in Boston where the network is headquartered. But I produce my shows with an engineer at the Washington bureau.

Under "N" and National Public Radio, I've got fourteen names. Some of these folks are with "Morning Edition;" others with "Weekend Edition" or "Weekend All Things Considered." There's a science editor, sports editor, deputy editor of the cultural desk.

Freelancing is all about contacts and people helping each other out – engineers, TV producers, radio station program directors, independent producers.

Over time many of the people I work with become friends. We talk about our kids, our travels, our lives. When my first child arrives, one of the first people I hear from is Jan Bailey, Acquisitions Director at Monitor Radio. Jan sends me a lovely letter saying how happy she is for my husband and me and our baby girl. I keep that letter in a special place.

ONE OF THE GREATS

I recall a day back in the 1970's driving my car around Hartford, madly changing channels on the radio trying to find some good music. I end up on a station where a man is giving a news report. While I can't recall the subject, I'm laughing when the broadcast ends and I'm thinking that I'd like to meet this newsman one day – this fellow named Charles Osgood.

Fast-forward twenty years. It sure would be great to work with Mr. Osgood on his famous show "The Osgood File." Calling his office at CBS in New York City, I reach Karen Beckers, his assistant, who for many years worked with Charles Kuralt. She puts me through to Mr. Osgood. Yes, he can meet with me, he says, just let him know the next time I'm in New York.

A couple weeks later entering his office at the CBS building on West 57th Street, I greet Charles Osgood and notice my audition tape in the cassette deck next to his desk. Looks like he listened to it. I'm thinking: "What now?" He tells me there is a way to get involved with his show, and that I need to contact a woman who heads an organization called American Communications Foundation. ACF acts as a go-between with CBS and independent radio producers. In our conversation Osgood also tells me that he worked at a station in Hartford before joining CBS. I learn that he lived on the same street where my grandparents had lived. It's a good meeting.

When back in New York several months later I call him again to see if he can join me for a cup of coffee. I have some story ideas to share with him. We end up walking a few blocks up the street for lunch at a restaurant called Biarritz, named after the beautiful seaside city in southwestern France.

During the meal, we talk mostly about "CBS News Sunday Morning," the network's popular TV show that Osgood also hosts. Charles loves music and plays piano and the harmonica. I suggest he invite Bob Dylan to the show and that they play their harmonicas together. For a moment Charles doesn't respond. But then points out that Dylan doesn't hold his harmonica when playing it. Oh, right. He's using his hands to play his guitar. His harmonica is attached to an apparatus in front of his head. Judging by Charles' reaction, I don't think he's very interested in my idea, so I don't pursue it any further.

We talk about other ideas, too – his and mine. It's fun at lunch hearing Charles impersonate Dan Rather when Rather was in China covering Richard Nixon's historic visit. Osgood's a good mimic and enjoys it. We talk a little about narrating and he offers me a tip – always imagine talking to one person, one face, he says, as it helps in sounding more natural. The food and wine taste especially good at this lunch with Charles Osgood.

A GREAT OPPORTUNITY

I follow up on Charles Osgood's suggestion for doing some work for The Osgood File and contact Cynthia Perry, who heads the American Communications Foundation. Perry oversees a group of independent producers like myself who want to contribute to Osgood's show.

ACF's routine is different from what I'm used to. Instead of coming up with my own idea for a show, ACF assigns me one. It's different from coming up with my own stories and the way I develop them. They choose the people to interview and do some pre-interviewing before handing me the story. Many interviews take place over the phone due to distances between the people involved. I've always been more comfortable holding a mic while standing next to a person. Then I can read their expressions and hear any inflection in their voice. It makes interviewing easier. Also, I like being able to veer off the subject from time to time if there's interesting or surprising information to be had. ACF editors discourage any surprises. They're committed to a particular focus for the piece.

After interviews I choose the sound bites for the show, then write a script, which is usually heavily edited by ACF editors. Finally, script and tape are sent to CBS where Charles Osgood's engineer, Phil Chin, mixes the piece. Charles writes his own introduction, and often makes his own last-minute edits to the script before he reads it on air. This adds the element of surprise for all of us producers and editors!

While Charles isn't always thrilled with the shows from ACF, he stays positive with his independent producers. We all get a tape of our program after it airs along with his and Phil's comments, and Cynthia Perry's at ACF, on whether they liked it, or what would have made it better.

I end up working on forty of Charles Osgood's shows.

In these four years (1996-2000), I learn a lot from Cynthia Perry, a strict and demanding editor. As a producer, I never send her any audiotape that is, in her words, 'muddy' i.e. not clear. Muddy is unacceptable – she's clear about that! She expects the best from her producers. I like working with her. She helps me organize stories better so they always have a beginning, middle and end. I tend sometimes to go in circles.

Though our paths never cross on her trips east from Mill Valley, outside of San Francisco, we talk on the phone a lot. I like picking up and hearing her familiar greeting, "Cynthia here." It usually means I've been assigned another story.

When Cynthia gets married, I'm vacationing in Maine and order four live lobsters shipped out to her in celebration of the event. What prompts me to send this particular gift, I don't know (maybe it's an obvious one, my being in Maine and all), but I'm glad I do. For it turns out she and her husband love lobster. In a great thank you note from her, I learn they feasted on a full lobster dinner then ate lobster rolls the next day. It makes me hungry just thinking about it.

FINANCES

I'm not making very much money with my feature work, but I'm talking with many interesting people and learning a lot. And I keep thinking that one day I'll be making more at this profession. I'm also thinking about maybe starting in TV, but my first opportunity requires a move to South Dakota. Apparently, a small media market in a small city in a less populated state is where I'd need to start. I've loved South Dakota ever since driving cross-country and seeing buffalo roaming wild in the Badlands. I liked, too, studying the faces of the four Presidents looking down at me from Mount Rushmore, and standing on a bridge in Pierre, the state capital, while watching a narrow, tame stretch of the Missouri River mosey along below. I think South Dakota would be a nice place to live, but with Buzz committed to a job he loves in Washington, we're not moving there anytime soon.

My radio feature stories pay me between $50 and $500 depending on the length of the show and the network that's buying it. On the other hand, a one-hour television narration for "Wild Discovery" pays $3000. I'm working to get some TV interest in my story ideas and begin writing proposals for TV documentaries using some of my radio show ideas and sending them off to Discovery Channel.

A friend at National Geographic Television gives me the name and phone number of a producer there to talk with about voice work. I reach him easily. He says that National Geographic is looking for another female narrator and thinks I can fit in. He says he'll call me back to follow-up. Time flies. There's no call. By the time I call him back to see if (rather than when) I can narrate a documentary for NG, he's retired. Bad luck, bad timing, or wishful thinking on my part? For most in the profession, life is busy and it's out of sight, out of mind. I should have called him back sooner and been more persistent, though there's a fine line between being persistent and pestering. With time, you learn that line. Still, you never want to hear the greeting, "Hello Stranger."

The Iraqi Tigers at half-time of a Peace Cup soccer game

Lucy Saner in Ennis, Montana relaxing before her interview
later at the Dinosaur Museum in Bozeman

Me with friend and guide Cal Riggs on the Snake River in
Idaho

Buzz Saner on the bank of the Madison River while guide
Bill Saunders retrieves gear from the boat

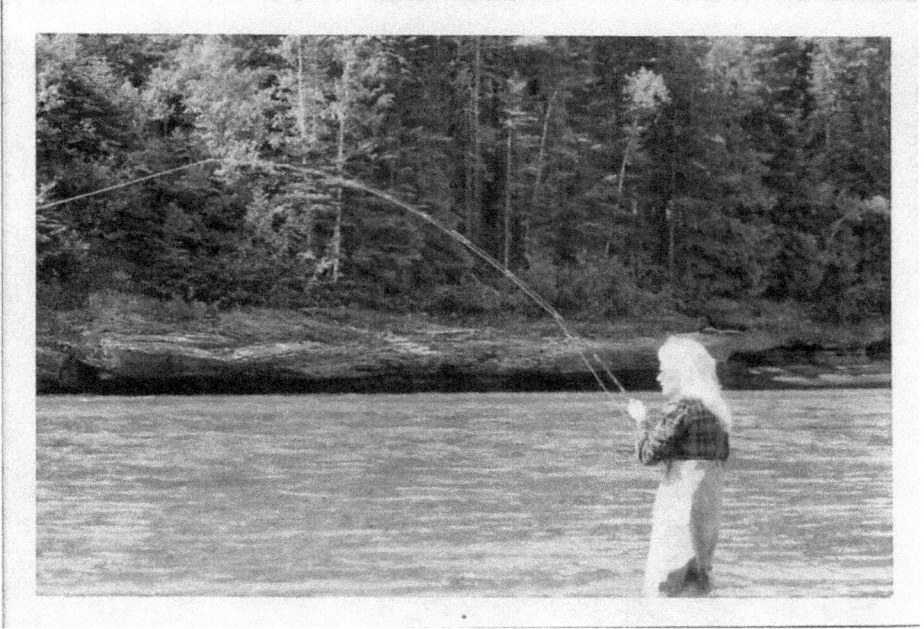

Atlantic salmon on the line on the St-Jean River on the
Gaspé Peninsula, Quebec

Charles Osgood and son, Winston, in southern France

Scottie's Shoe Store (and emporium: note the range of
merchandise), Chestertown, MD

Leigh Saner with blueberries she picked atop
Mt. Megunticook in Maine

Women on Wheels

Women on Wheels stop for lunch in Rock Hall, MD

The luncheon party at Cremona Farm
Left to right: Walter Deshler, Bryan Fick,
Steve Purvins, Nick Ferrante, Norton Dodge

Thatcher, Colin McGhee

PART TWO

CHESTERTOWN, MARYLAND

When Buzz and I decide to move with our two young daughters out of DC to a quieter place, I remember Chestertown. Ever since passing through it on route to Echo Hill, the town has been in the back of my mind. Since Buzz has never seen it, we drive out on a weekend in the spring to have lunch and look around.

Chestertown is an old-fashioned town. More than 300 years old, it was settled on the Chester River, a tributary of the Chesapeake Bay. On the town's north side is Washington College, named after George Washington, the only college he loaned his name to and served on its Board of Sponsors. It is the tenth oldest college in the country.

Driving into town this Saturday morning, a crowd of people walk through the farmers' market that's set up on the town square. There's a steady stream of folks going in and out of the coffee shop and a pharmacy that serves up ice cream cones and milk shakes. We stop into Scottie's, a shoe store that also sells newspapers, magazines, penny candy, postcards and American Girl Doll clothes. Three men are sitting near the front door chatting. Outside people walk by and greet one another. As we leave the store, a woman drives by, honks and waves. I wave back, then realize she's waving to a lady in front of me. But seeing me wave, she waves again, this time to me. I may have just made a new friend. The town has a nice feel to it – friendly, relaxed. It isn't long before we decide to move to Chestertown.

Soon after settling down on Maryland's Eastern Shore, I'm back searching for new stories. I'm thinking too about taking up motorcycling again – thinking that it will be a lot safer here than in the city.

MOTORCYCLE SAFETY CLASS

When I sign up for motorcycle safety class I'm not thinking at all about turning my experience into a radio show. But by the second class, I know it's a great subject. I call a producer at NPR and get approval for a piece on spec. Now I need permission from the manager of the motorcycle program and the class instructor. When they consent, I'm ready to go.

In producing this story, I have two roles to perform – I'm a student riding a motorcycle in a class, and a radio producer recording what the instructor and my classmates are thinking and doing. It's challenging, in part because it splits my focus between what I'm trying to take in as a professional journalist and what I'm trying to take in as a student. Logistics are a challenge, too. At times, I'm off my bike taping our teacher's directions to the class. Then I need to put my radio equipment on the ground, jump onto my bike and ride with my class, following the instructions.

For the interviews, I seek out the quiet of my car. Classmates take turns sitting in the passenger seat as I record their clear, easy-to-hear answers to my questions.

Walter Watson, NPR's Producer/Director of "Weekend All Things Considered," isn't sold on my show until I arrive at NPR studios with my tape. Associate Producer, Fred Wasser, listens to it first. The sounds of motorcycles revving and rumbling and instructor Bernard Johnson barking commands is throbbing and exciting. Wasser knows it. He calls in Walter to listen.

All day (minus a short break for a snack) I'm at NPR studios. Fred and Walter are in and out of the room where I'm at work selecting sound bites and ambience, then writing the copy. When Walter makes an edit, he always asks me if I'm okay with it. Each time I am, and they're made. Then he gives me some advice on writing. Whenever I'm having trouble with a sentence, he tells me to say what I mean out loud, then write it down. I try it and find the sentence.

At the end of the day, with my edited copy in hand, I'm ready to narrate the show, and join Fred Wasser and an engineer in the studio. I'm reluctant to dissect the story any further, so here is the show.

"Motorcycle Safety Class Rekindles Love Of Riding For Reporter"
Weekend All Things Considered, August 20, 2000

(Reprinted with permission from National Public Radio, Inc.)

JACKI LYDEN, host:

When she was a college kid in the early 1970s, reporter Mary Saner rode a motorcycle, but she always felt a bit too wild. Now, after attending a motorcycle class, she's rediscovered the thrill and camaraderie of motorcycling.

SOUNDBITE OF MOTORCYCLE ENGINE

Mr. BERNARD JOHNSON(ph)(Instructor): OK. Head and eyes up. Knees to the tank. Now remember to do a head check when you go across ...(unintelligible} turn. Knees to the tank. Nice constant acceleration throughout the turn.

MARY SANER reporting:

Even before walking into motorcycle safety class, I envisioned myself and 10 teenaged guys riding our bikes together, but that's not quite the case. Some of us who'd ridden before shared motorcycle stories, some were harrowing. In some of the riding exercises, we needed to make eye contact with each other and follow body language on the bikes, a nod or a wink. We soon felt like friends.

I'm not the oldest in the riding class, nor the only woman. This course used to be the exclusive domain of men, at least in southern Maryland. Bernard Johnson, my instructor, tells me he's seen a change.

Mr. JOHNSON: Well, I'll tell you what I've found in the last eight years. I've found a lot more females coming through. They're tired of being passengers. They want to become riders.

SANER: By the third time we're on the bikes, everyone out here is looking more relaxed. I feel comfortable with my bike. I know where all the controls are, the throttle's in the right hand, and I have a better feel for it now. I'm not looking down. I'm looking ahead. I'm not worrying as much. Riding is coming back to me, not only the shifting and accelerating, but that feeling that makes you want to laugh out loud.

Lori Smith(ph), a woman in my class, manages a bank. She says biking makes her feel the same way.

Ms. LORI SMITH (Biker): It's a freedom and you're out there and it's just--you can't describe it. There's a T-shirt: If I have to explain it, you wouldn't understand. But when you're riding down the road on a bike and you see bikes, they wave to each other. You know, they can be on opposite ends of the highway passing and they'll wave. It's just a common bond that people have the love of riding.

SANER: Ever since we moved out of the city and back to a small town, I wanted to get a motorcycle to ride on these beautiful country roads. It's been 25 years since I got off my 125 Yamaha. That's a small bike. It seemed like the right time and place for a motorcycle class. In Salisbury, Maryland, I joined 10 kindred spirits, most of them longing to get in touch with their inner Hell's Angel.

Mr. JOHNSON: Start your engines.

SOUNDBITE OF MOTORCYCLE ENGINES STARTING

SANER: My heart jumped a little on that first command. I hadn't felt an engine rumbling beneath me in a long time, at least not a Honda.

Mr. JOHNSON: Two feet under. There you go. Ease into your friction zone.

SOUNDBITE OF ENGINE REVVING

Mr. JOHNSON: Head and eyes up. Way to go. Cover your clutch.

SANER: Another woman in the class, Cindy Parks(ph), is used to riding on the bike of her husband's motorcycle, but at 46 she says she wants to learn how to handle a bike in case her husband gets hurt or sick when they're out on the road. But these riding lessons are more than she's bargained for. Cindy sums up her feelings in three little words.

Ms. CINDY PARKS (Biker): Scared to death.

SANER: She didn't exactly look like she was made for biking, but that didn't stop her.

Ms. PARKS: I didn't know if I'd be able to stay up on the thing, because I had an experience when I was a teen-ager that was not very good for a two-wheeled motorized vehicle.

SANER: Did you go over or...

Ms. PARKS: No. I tried to drive the thing up a mailbox. I went across the front yard and up the mailbox. I stood there holding the handlebars saying, 'How do I cut this thing off?'

SANER: Unlike Cindy, I'd never had an accident on a motorcycle. Not because of my skills, that's for sure, more like sheer luck. But here, the class of 2000 were straddling our Honda 250 Rebels. Both Cindy and I learned a lot about each other. We both have kids who thought biking was a great idea. My eight- and 12-year-old daughters finally think I'm kind of cool. Cindy tells me she's impressed her kids in a way.

Ms. PARKS: Well, we haven't had our bike very long and our daughter, at the time, I think she was about 17 or 18, said we were going through a mid-life crisis.

SANER: My kids' friends said the same thing. I said, 'Hey, you know, they may be right.'

Ms. PARKS: Well, we're having a good time.

SOUNDBITE OF ENGINE REVVING

SANER: A scary good time. There's an incredible thrust with a motorcycle. It's like the engine has a mind of its own. Jose Gutierrez(ph) has ridden bikes before, and when he isn't on his monster bike, he tracks weather satellites for a living. Jose is 50. In class, he smiles with confidence. When I tell him he looks like he's born to ride, he doesn't believe it.

Mr. JOSE GUTIERREZ (Biker): I am having a very difficult time keeping the bike going as slow as a lot of the riders on the course.

SANER: And that's why it's difficult. When I move the throttle ever so slightly, there's a huge surge of power and noise. It's exciting. That instant speed is what it's all about. But if you don't pay attention, you're in big trouble, fast. On quick stops, if I don't brake properly or keep my balance just right, the bike could fall over. It's never happened to me, but I saw one classmate who was riding his bike up to load it onto a trailer at the end of the class. He hit the throttle instead of the brake. He swerved and lost control. The bike fell on top of him. The bike was still revving with him pinned underneath. It was the only accident in our seven-day course. Just moments before, Bernard, our teacher, told us to stay seated on our bikes until we were all parked and our engines off. He said we were much safer atop the bikes, and he was right.

It was just a week. I really loved going to Motorcycle Safety Class, because riding was fun and my classmates were all different. There was a father and a son, an electrician, a couple of college students, a mail carrier, the owner of a construction company. There was this feeling we all shared, this one common interest: the freedom, the friendship, a thrill that you can only get when you're there. The last day of class we exchanged phone numbers. We talked about a reunion ride. My husband isn't opposed to my riding. He's just a little worried about the dangers and all. But I'm going to buy a bike soon and maybe I'll get him a sidecar.

SOUNDBITE OF MOTORCYCLES

LYDEN: Mary Saner lives to ride in Maryland.

SOUNDBITE OF MUSIC

##

Postscript

Some listeners write in after hearing the program. There's a postcard from a former Dean of my college. She liked the show but is a little worried about the safety of motorcycling. Then an email arrives from a member of Women on Wheels (WOW) who wants me to join a local chapter in Salisbury, Maryland and ride with her and other WOW members. I'll later produce a radio feature and a magazine article about Women on Wheels. And there's a man in Maine who writes to tell me about riding a motorcycle in college in the 1970's and returning to biking last year while in his late 40's. He says, "Your story captured the essence of rediscovering the joy of riding. I often ride to work on my bike (a 750cc, a lot bigger than my bike in college), and I often think that motorcycles are the reason God made summer mornings in Maine.

THE CAT RESORT

My sister, Ginny Hilyard, has a pronounced creative streak and is always full of ideas (see Mall Walking story). During a vacation in Maine, she tells me about a place up the road from our house in Camden. It's called the Cat Resort. People drop their cats off there when going on vacation. It costs $9.50 a night. A fellow named Richard Wilson runs the place. I give him a call to see if I can stop by sometime and talk to him about doing a radio show. Five minutes on the phone with Mr. Wilson convinces me this will be a great feature. He's fun and an authority on cats. So, I phone an editor at NPR who goes along with my idea for a story. (I later learn that several editors wanted to be assigned this piece).

At "Pussies Port of Call" (the official name of the cat resort), cats live in "condos" three feet by five feet. They lounge in a rocking chair, watch videos, play on a jungle gym and gaze out the window at birds, animals and lobster boats passing by on Penobscot Bay.

Richard Wilson knows more about cats than anyone I've ever met and perhaps more than anyone else. He shows me around the resort while talking to the guests – Dervis, Shakespeare and Luke, among others. The cats have their idiosyncrasies, he says, and then tells me about two cats who are long-time guests and who prefer a particular condo (an ocean front, I think). When they're taken to a different one they stop and confront the cat in 'their' condo. Wilson says, "They just stood in front of the other cat and said, 'What are you doing in our unit?' and looked back at us like, 'Hey, get her out of here.'"

Mrs. Wilson helps her husband with the business and talks about special diets and general health care of the cats. Then a cat owner stops in to pick up his cat and there's a third (human) voice to go with the other animal ones. It's ideal. For radio, it's the cat's meow.

Produced three different shows for NPR, Voice of America and Westwood One Radio Network.

RIVERTON

When doing interviews for radio features, I pretty much work alone. But then there are times when my family gets drawn into the action.

I think back on a trip to Riverton, Connecticut with my daughter, Leigh, then age ten. I'm at work on a series for Voice of America about small towns in America. Riverton is a quiet, colonial village on the picturesque Farmington River. Once a stagecoach stop on the Hartford to Albany route, Riverton now attracts people from all over the country who want to fish the Farmington and stay in the comfortable, historic Riverton Inn.

Leigh has swimming and eating ice cream in mind for this trip.

In the early morning, standing in hip boots out near the middle of the river, I find a fisherman to interview. He tells me he loves the Farmington – that it's supposed to be the cleanest river in New England, and it's full of trout. While he's seen some fish jumping downstream, he hasn't hooked one here yet. After the interview, I tape some background sound of him wading in the current. But I don't think to check and make sure the sound is good until after he's disappeared downstream. On the playback, the tape doesn't sound at all like water – just turbulence. No way I'll be able to use it in my show. Looking over at Leigh sitting on the bank, I wade ashore.

"Can you walk around some in the water for me?" I ask.

"Sure."

In her already soggy sneakers, she slides off the bank and heads out over slippery rocks, splashing as she goes.

All the while I'm recording clear, useable sound of being in the current of the Farmington River. Thank you, Leigh! Let's take a swim and get some ice cream!

COCKTAIL CONVERSATION

Cocktail parties don't lend themselves to conversations of great depth, which suits me fine. I can talk on most any subject for five to ten minutes – a little longer than a feature story, but not much.

Sometimes my family can't take it. They want to tell me something that I don't already know. But since I'm reading two to three newspapers a day and every magazine I can get my hands on to get ideas for programs about art, science, health, religion, sports, human interest, entertainment, music, etc., I feel like I know a little something about everything. That's what feature work can do to you.

When I tell people what I do, they always respond positively:

"That must be the perfect job!"

Yes, if you don't count the pay, the hours, the driving and a few other things.

"You've got a niche."

True, I only know one other person who does this fulltime – and she just quit.

"What's been your favorite story?"

The last one I did.

"How long will you do this?"

Forever. It's what I do best, and I'm addicted, or at least dependent.

AN AGENT

Do I need an agent to find me more voice work? I continually ask myself that question. Yes, I think I do. Locating a list of agents who represent independent producers, I pick out the firm of Oppenheim Christie in New York City and call their office and set up a meeting with Arnie Christie.

Entering the office of Oppenheim Christie isn't especially memorable except for the phone ringing. Luckily, I don't have to record an interview here. I like Arnie Christie right away. He's businesslike, friendly and interested in the work I'm doing, and he asks me the obvious question: Wouldn't having an agent in Washington be a better idea – the convenience and all? I'm thinking Yes but say No. After all, I'm here and he seems interested in getting me some work.

Handing him the same audition tape that got me my first job with Discovery Channel, he promises to listen and try and find a commercial for me to voice. While there's no formal agreement, no papers signed, I walk out of his office encouraged – and crossing my fingers.

When the phone rings one fall afternoon and it's an associate of Oppenheim Christie, I'm happily surprised. The fellow wants to know if I can voice a commercial tomorrow in New York City. It will pay $50. As he talks I'm calculating traveling costs to New York and back on the train. It's about $125 – and then there's getting around the city. I'll lose money on the venture. While I could juggle my appointments the next day, I decide not to take the job. It's a mistake. Looking back, I should have gone to New York and absorbed the financial loss. I would have gotten some experience and built up my resume. Of course, a freelancer needs to be able to do more than breakeven – this is not a hobby – but at the same time, you need to weigh the potential longer-term benefits and possibilities, and sometimes, you just go for it.

FIREWORKS

Living in a college town has its advantages – like having professors nearby and available for interviews. As the Fourth of July approaches, I'm considering a show on fireworks. A producer at Westwood One Radio Network wants me to pursue it.

I call my friend John Buettner in the Public Relations office at Washington College to see if he can recommend someone for an interview on fireworks. It turns out that Chemistry Professor John Conkling is also the Director of the American Pyrotechnic Association.

"It's the Mother Lode!" says John in an email.

Science can be complicated. In radio, it's a must that it not be. A listener must never be confused. He or she doesn't have the luxury as in anything you read, to go back over something that was even slightly confusing. Not to worry, Dr. Conkling is a master at simplifying the science of fireworks. Vividly he describes how he safely experiments with various chemical elements – some produce light; some sound; some propulsion. In his lab, he shows me his fume hood, which looks like a small oven, where he tests the chemicals. It's noisy and exciting.

What is especially fun about this show is finding out that someone's heard it. Our neighbor, John Wayne, who also happens to know a lot about pyrotechnics, tells me he woke up to his radio and the sounds of me and his friend John Conkling talking. Having feedback from my shows is good. Any feedback, in my mind, is good feedback.

NARRATION GONE WRONG

A question not asked can make the difference between success and failure. One morning while producing a show with engineer Bob Doughty at Voice of America, a producer for another VOA program walks into the studio to check on a time to record his show. He's also looking for someone to voice the piece. "Mary would be great," says Bob. "She could do it after we finish this."

I'm nodding – yes, great idea, and how do you do.

The producer hands me the copy. It's for a show about Lady Gaga. It looks simple – one page – about a minute's worth of narration. Before the producer leaves the studio saying he'll be back soon, he reads a few lines of it to illustrate a point that I now can't recall. But he reads with no inflection, no variance, no rhythm – like he's reading a grocery list. I mistake it for the style he wants in the narration, and rather than ask a question about it or ask Bob, who's now busy talking to another producer who has just entered the studio, I let it go. Big mistake. My read is terrible. Bob looks perplexed during it, but only corrects me when I mispronounce David Bowie's name (Bowee" he says, not Boohee).

I figure out my mistake days later when the show doesn't air and I'm not paid. It's a big let-down, and another lesson learned the hard way. ALWAYS ask the question even if it seems like a stupid one.

NEAR DEATH EXPERIENCE

As far as I know, my radio feature on Near Death Experience (NDE) airs before any books appear on the subject. Over the course of several years I've been talking to a friend who has studied NDE and knows people who've experienced the phenomenon. It's an intriguing subject, to say the least, and I have little trouble in selling the idea for a show to editor Faith Lapidus at Voice of America.

Family friend, Reverend David LaMotte, Sr., who gives talks on NDE's locally, gives me the contact information for William Taylor. He knows Taylor and all about Taylor's experience with NDE. In a phone call Bill Taylor invites me to join him and a group of others in a meeting that he will lead. I'm quickly on my way with this story.

I interview Reverend LaMotte while sitting beside him on the back porch of his home named "Friendship." I'm struck by his open mindedness about religion and can see why so many people have shared with him their experiences, thoughts and questions about Near Death Experience. He's a very good listener and is a firm believer in NDE.

Recently VOA has begun transforming features, once they have aired, into articles that are posted on the network's website. The articles include photographs. Using photos has made my job harder since now I not only record interviews, but also take pictures of the people in them. On the plus side, millions of folks around the world visit VOA's website and see the articles.

Here is the transcript of my show on NDE for Voice of America:

DATE=
TYPE=English Programs Feature
NUMBER=
TITLE=Near Death Experience
BYLINE=Mary Saner
TELEPHONE=410 778-7646
DATELINE=Columbia, Maryland
EDITOR=Faith Lapidus
CONTENT=

INTRO: There are some things that cannot be explained - by science or any other means. The near death experience remains an inexplicable and astonishing phenomenon. Mary Saner reports.

TEXT: As many as 13 million people in the United States claim to have had what's known as a near death experience. They were critically close to death ... or were actually declared clinically dead - they weren't breathing, and had no heartbeat- but then, they regained consciousness. Their accounts of what happened during that event are strikingly similar.

TAPE: CUT ONE - WILLIAM TAYLOR
"One of the characteristics is being out of body, a viewing of their body from another perspective. In medical situations, they perhaps find themselves floating on the ceiling looking back down on the operating table and seeing the doctors and nurses working on them."

TEXT: 61-year-old William Taylor had a near death experience that he says dramatically changed his life.

TAPE: CUT TWO-BILL TAYLOR
"In 1979 I had a cardiac arrest and went into the local hospital and then up to Hopkins in Baltimore. I coded 3 times - coded means that your heart stops or your breathing stops. I was revived 3 times. The essence of what I experienced was I suddenly found myself way out in space, and I could look back and see how everything is connected to everything else. There's just a warmth. I didn't have an extremely bright light, but I could see light in everything. I still could experience and think, 'Wow, I'm still here. I'm still separate and I can still think."

TEXT: Mr. Taylor says he made the decision to live.

TAPE: CUT THREE - BILL TAYLOR
"There was a very powerful being there and this being said, 'It's your choice.' My mother and my father were alive and they were at the hospital, and this being told me, 'Before you make this choice, put your hand,' - I'm in spirit form here -' put your hand on your mother's heart and also put your hand on my heart.' And I think when I did that, I felt her pain would I have died - would I not have come back."

TEXT: But, like many who encounter near-death, Mr. Taylor says it was difficult to talk about his experience afterwards, because no one believed him.

TAPE: CUT FOUR- BILL TAYLOR
"I told my cardiologist and he said that we really can't explain this and there's no reason that we need to discuss it any further. And my family was not real happy to hear about it either. Since then, reading some of the literature, it's oftentimes most difficult to talk about it with family and close friends. A total stranger is oftentimes more easy to converse with because a family, I guess they see you in a particular light and they expect you to behave in a certain way."

TEXT: 14 years after his heart attack, William Taylor joined the International Association of Near Death Studies. IANDS offers information and a forum for people to talk and listen.

TAPE: CUT FIVE - AMBIENCE OF OPENING OF MEETING - (BELL RINGING)
"Welcome everybody. This is the Maryland Chapter of the International Association of Near Death Studies. Today, we thought we'd look at a video and then open for discussion later on."

TEXT: After watching the video featuring nurse and IANDS Board member, Debbie James, the 11 men and women seated around the long table begin to talk.

TAPE: CUTS SIX AND SEVEN - MONTAGE OF LARRY AND WOMAN

(Woman) "I have not shared my experiences much. I haven't. I'm afraid of giving them up." (Larry) "My experience was so precious to me that it was only when I started coming here about 2 years ago that I told my story. My wife asked me why are you going to this group? And I said, ' Well, you know, I had that experience in India.' She said, 'I don't know what you're talking about' and evidently I'd never told her about it."

TEXT: 80-year-old Larry Bott comes to many IANDS meetings. At this one, he relates his near death experience 20 years ago.

TAPE: CUT EIGHT - LARRY BOTT
"I was trekking in the Western Himalayas and went back to New Delhi, wandered around the streets of Old Delhi, got very sick and was in my hotel room and I started experiencing music. It sounded like a choir.

TEXT: Then, he says, he saw something that was vivid and unforgettable.

TAPE: CUT NINE - LARRY BOTT
"I watched from the corner of my hotel room at myself at one point. The manager of the hotel had come in the room and was shaking me, and it was so disturbing. I was enjoying myself so thoroughly. He shook me, and I spoke to him and said, 'why are you shaking me?' I looked down on the bed and said, ' I'm just fine."

TEXT: But Mr. Bott was not fine. He had lost 20 kilos from dehydration and was suffering from bacillary dysentery. He was brought to the intensive care unit at a hospital in New Delhi and eventually recovered. Mr. Bott says he is enjoying life, and has no fear of death.
    Many in the religious and medical communities are unsure of what the near-death experience means. But not David LaMotte.

TAPE: CUT TEN - REVEREND DAVID LAMOTTE
"Through 25 years now of my studies, I think this is the most exciting and important revelation, if you want to call it that, that has ever come to earth."

TEXT: The Protestant minister has spoken with about a dozen people who've had a near- death experience and has read accounts of hundreds of others. He says near-death experience has extraordinary importance for spiritual thought.

TAPE: CUT ELEVEN - REVEREND DAVID LAMOTTE
"It has meaning for everyone, everywhere, in every possible way. This particular occasion of near-death experience comes to Christians, Jews, Muslims, Buddhists, Hindus, pure atheists."

TEXT: Mr. LaMotte has been studying near-death experience to help him respond to his parishioners' questions and fears about death. And, he says, from what he's seen and learned, many of those who've experienced near-death view life differently than the rest of us.

TAPE: CUT TWELVE - DAVID LAMOTTE
"They are open spiritually to practically anything that is good. Love and knowledge. And they believe that all of us are related and that life is beautiful, no matter what part of the world you're in, no matter what race or religion - we're all related in the beauty and love of the Almighty."

TAPE: CUT THIRTEEN - DR. GEORGE YOUNG
"I don't know what this is, and I would think it may be actually something going wrong because of lack of blood flow to certain parts of your brain."

TEXT: Cardiologist George Young is a skeptic. Many near death experiences occur during cardiac arrest, and Dr. Young says the body's response to a heart attack could be responsible for some of the common phenomena of near-death experiences. For example, the bright light many people claim to see could involve brain cells firing off as they die.

TAPE: CUT FOURTEEN - DR. GEORGE YOUNG AND SANER
"You can actually see that with an MRI. (You mean the cells firing off?) Willy-nilly, all over the place, and you might be able to get from the optic neurons a very big firing off. It's like a light bulb that pops when it burns out. It could be that phenomenon."

TEXT: He says the euphoria that many claim to feel during near death might simply be the effect of pain-killing endorphins being released in the brain. But for the other common symptoms -- the sense of passing through a tunnel, floating outside the body, meeting deceased relatives - no medical explanations have been offered. Many scientific studies are underway to what happens during near-death, and in the meantime, William Taylor has a message for those who haven't experienced it.

TAPE: CUT FIFTEEN - BILL TAYLOR

"It would be good if people could retain an open mind and not put things down just because they don't understand it or science can't explain it. Remain open to it a little bit. Perhaps it is possible. Maybe there really is a heaven. Maybe that's really where we go. Maybe we don't really die. Just think about some of that."

TEXT: The International Association of Near Death Studies has about one thousand members around the world. It offers information and resources about the experience on its website - iands-dot-org.

For "Our World" I'm Mary Saner in Columbia, Maryland.

Reprinted with permission from Voice of America

Postscript

Reverend David LaMotte died on June 24, 2006. I remember that night well. There was a storm like none I have ever seen before. The sky was alight as if it was daytime, but there was no thunder or rain. I could see for miles in the brilliant flashes. To me, Reverend LaMotte was going to heaven.

So many people came to his memorial service that there was no more room in the church. A crowd of us stood outside and listened to the loud speaker that piped out the words of his family and the minister. I talked with people there of all ages – some were married by him, some baptized; some both. All of us were his friends.

MORE NARRATION

I have this feeling that reminds me of William Hurt in the movie "Broadcast News." In the movie Hurt is a news anchor who sometimes doesn't entirely understand what he's reading.

The Discovery Channel program "Phantom Tiger" is about the Tasmanian tiger – the last official sighting being sixty years ago. But that hasn't stopped recent sightings by people who swear the tiger still exists.

When I receive the 19-page script, I notice my narration is short. The show's dialogue consists mostly of historians, scientists, tiger hunters and others. Skimming through the text, I concentrate on rehearsing my own voice-over sections. But when the time comes to tape the show in Discovery's studio, I wish I'd studied the whole text more carefully. Not being that familiar with all the facts in the script makes me a little less comfortable reading my part. Maybe knowledge affects confidence in a voice – I don't know– but while my read turns out fine, I think it could have been better.

ULTRALIGHTS

Unfortunately, I've never been good at making things or fixing them. So, reading an article about people who build themselves an airplane captures my imagination. Ultralights are lightweight hand-built airplanes. They weigh less than 254 pounds. The engine is often taken from a lawn mower or snowmobile.

In this piece pilot Ray Gefken is a strong interview. Among other things he tells me about landing his plane in someone's driveway and taxiing up the driveway to their front door to deliver some pictures. But Faith Lapidus at Voice of America insists on an extra voice for the show – an extra interview for depth. This creates a lot more work, but the show improves with the addition of Jeanette Smolinski.

Here is my feature on ultralights. As in all VOA programs, measurements are in the metric system:

>   115 kilos = 254 pounds
>   100 kilometers per hour = 62 miles an hour
>   19 liters = 5 gallons

TITLE=Ultralights
BYLINE=Mary Saner
DATELINE=Weirwood, Virginia
NUMBER=

INTRO: A lot of people drive cars. Fewer have flown in planes. Even fewer have built their own plane. Mary Saner has the story.

TEXT: Near a grassy airstrip on the Eastern Shore of Virginia, Ray Gefken is checking the wings and wheels of his plane. Gefken flies an ultralight - a single seat airplane with a tiny cockpit and engine.

AUDIO: AMBIENCE OF GEFKEN PULLING THE CORD AND STARTNG THE ENGINE

AUDIO: CUT ONE- RAY GEFKEN

"This particular engine - I call it the "Armstrong" method. It's a pull starter just like an old outboard motor type thing or a lawn mower."

TEXT: The 74-year-old businessman has been a licensed pilot for 35 years. But you don't need a license to fly ultralights. They weigh less than 115 kilos, Their top speed is just over 100 kilometers per hour, though many fly slower. People who fly these bare- bones planes often build them from kits.

Jeanette Smolinski, a computer systems engineer, got interested in building an ultralight the first time she saw one.

AUDIO: CUT TWO – JEANETTE SMOLINSKI

"My neighbor moved here more than 40 years ago and he flew a Cessna at the time. And it became too expensive so he investigated and found this ultralight called a CGS Hawk. So if you can imagine, he would take off and fly and I could hear him - I could hear the sound as he came above the tree line, and then he would just circle around before he'd go wherever, and I would stand out there and look at it and say 'you know what, I can do that, too.'

TEXT: So Smolinski bought an ultralight kit. Then, in her garage, she built the plane with her father.

AUDIO: CUT THREE-JEANETTE SMOLINSKI

"How many daughters get that kind of fun with their father? It was an amazing event. In winter we would be out here working, in summer we would be out here working."

TEXT: It took Smolinski two years to build the plane in her spare time. Then her neighbor took her up in his small plane and taught her how to fly it. She also practiced by using the controls on the ground - - and learned more by feel.

AUDIO: CUT FOUR - JEANETTE SMOLINSKI

"You take little hops on the runway and from the hops then you might get just a wee bit airborne, but then you have to learn how to put it back down before you get to the end of the runway and practice that way."

TEXT: After about 30 hours of training, Smolinski says she felt ready for her first real flight.

AUDIO: CUT FIVE - JEANETTE SMOLINSKI

"In the plane I go full throttle - takeoff - the engine is at its full capacity until I reached an altitude of 1200 (feet). Then I pulled the throttle back and leveled her off and looked down, and my heart just leapt through my throat, and I had to do some self-talking at this point and say 'you're fine, it's not just going to fall out of the sky, you're fine.' I flew around. About a half hour later I came in for my first landing by myself."

AUDIO: CUT SIX- RAY GEFKEN

"There's an old saying -takeoffs are optional but landings are mandatory. It's easy to get a plane into the air, but it's more difficult to land it because you have to coordinate everything at the right time. The plane has to stop flying right at the spot where you want to land. Taking off, you just floor the throttle and off it goes. But coming back, you have to make the spot where you want to land - and that takes practice, that's all."

TEXT: Unlike other private planes, ultralights do not have to be registered with the Federal Aviation Administration....so there's no official record of how many there are. But the Experimental Aircraft Association estimates that there are hundreds of ultralight pilots across the country. Federal regulations restrict their flights to daylight hours and clear weather. And they may only fly in unpopulated areas.
The most gasoline they're allowed to carry is 19 liters. But the limitations don't seem to bother ultralight fans.

AUDIO: AMBIENCE OF PLANE

TEXT: On this warm and sunny spring day, Ray Gefken swings his plane around and accelerates down the runway, lifting off into a blue sky. A gust of wind tips his wings as he banks to the west towards the Chesapeake Bay. He says, "It's like floating on air."

For VOA News, I'm Mary Saner in Weirwood, Virginia
Reprinted with permission from Voice of America

Postscript

When I'm taping a story in a place more than three hours away, I often spend the night there. That's the case with this piece. I ask Ray Gefken for suggestions on where to stay and eat. He recommends the Best Western not far from the airstrip, and the diner next door, which he likes a lot. It's a stellar recommendation. After a long day of interviewing, I drop my bags at the motel and walk across the parking lot to Sage Diner. I'm tired, hungry and thirsty. When I order a Chardonnay, the waitress brings over a large glass filled to the brim. It's tasty and costs about $3.75. Then comes the catch of the day – fried drum caught a few hours ago, she says, in the Atlantic Ocean, just a couple miles east of here. I learn that a male drum often makes a drumming sound when mating. The drum is also a good eating fish. It hits the spot. All is well tonight on the Eastern Shore of Virginia. My only concern is whether to order the lemon meringue pie or, maybe, the coconut cream?

ARTICLES

Converting parts of my radio stories into articles for local magazines squeezes a little more life and a little more money out of them. The following article is inspired by one of my shows for Voice of America concerning the growth of vineyards and winemaking in Maryland.

A gentleman named Norton Dodge has graciously invited me to lunch on his Maryland estate where he's sharing homemade wine with friends. There's some War of 1812 history here, as well as humor.

For some reason, I put this article aside maybe to concentrate on other projects. It is never published. Even so, it was pure pleasure to research and write.

A Wine Affair to Remember

It is a scene worthy of an Impressionist painting – a luncheon party of five gentlemen on a grand Tidewater estate alongside the historic Patuxent River. A party under a huge shade tree with red wine from the farm's small vineyard, sandwiches on thick crusted bread, and salty black-eyed peas.

I arrive at Cremona Farm with Steve Purvins, a St. Mary's County farmer, who owns a small vineyard nearby. Steve wants me to meet someone more experienced than he is in growing grapes in southern Maryland, so he has invited me to lunch with Walter Deshler. Mr. Deshler, 84, who looks more like 60, is a good friend of Norton Dodge, who owns this beautiful estate with its 200-year old brick manor house. Deshler and Dodge, once professors at the University of Maryland, have been producing wine here for 35 years as a hobby. Their wine is bottled with the label *Cremona*.

Mr. Dodge, in his late 70's and with an ever-present smile, asks me to have a seat at his long picnic table. Then while pouring me a cup of red wine tells the story of his land, which was once a tobacco farm dating back to 1658.

"In the War of 1812 when the British invaded Washington and burned the Capitol, they came up the Patuxent River right past here, because the Potomac was too well protected with forts. This route was the approach from the soft underbelly. The British landed their cavalry right down here a mile or two and the infantry up above some five miles. And then they marched to Bladensburg for the battle there. In the Battle of Bladensburg, the Americans retreated rapidly to Washington."

Where the British pillaged then set fire to the White House.

Mr. Dodge has lived here almost 40 years and explains that his interest in winemaking started under a mulberry tree.

"I'd acquired this place and saw an awful lot of mulberries cascading out of trees and thought there must be some way of using them. And all I produced was vinegar. Walter said, 'Why don't you grow grapes?' So, we decided we'd get some of the shoots you start with and we got in a couple of acres."

Walter Deshler laughs. "That was the easiest part of it. You can plant a couple acres in a day. A big thrill. Then it all goes downhill after that. But we're still speaking."

Mr. Dodge says their wine is for family and friends, though in years of good production, they sell some grapes to people who want to make wine.

Another distinguished guest at the picnic table today is Nick Ferrante. Mr. Ferrante who's slight and smiles from under his white hat, sells a variety of wines at his family-owned grocery stores around Washington.

"I'm a friend and come here just to drink their wines, and then I give them a piece of my mind on what I think of them," he laughs. "But I think they're doing a good job. I believe in blending wines…but Walter doesn't believe in blending the different grapes, but we get along fine. We enjoy one another."

Mr. Ferrante has brought with him a bottle of 1996 Cremona, a gift a few years back from Mr. Deshler. He says he's been using it as a rolling pin.

"Yesterday I was rolling some dough and I couldn't find a rolling pin, so I got the bottle of wine, took the labels off and rolled the dough. Then I thought, if this is good enough to roll, it's good enough to drink. So, I opened the bottle and it was super! So, I brought it today."

Norton Dodge nods. "It's a very well-rounded wine."

The Cremona Vineyard is smaller these days, about one and a half acres, but it's an example to local grape growers in this burgeoning industry of how wine was once made. Steve Purvins says he's learned a lot from his friends at Cremona Farm.

"To come here, especially during the crush, is really nice. They bring all their children and in some cases their children's children," Purvins says, "and in the morning, we pick grapes and then at lunch time we all come down here to the water and everybody brings a dish and we all have lunch. Then it's back to the winery, and everybody gets to participate. The little kids, they like to crank the hand crusher. Then we sit around the press and people operate the press and pour the wine off. And, of course, there's always some workers' wine. It's really a nice family event."

LUNCH AT ELLEN'S

It's not just ordering quickly and getting the food sooner, but rather the conversation that makes sitting at the counter of Ellen's Coffee Shop in my hometown of Chestertown so good. I turn a lunch counter experience into an article for a local publication called *"Chesapeake Times."*

Here's the article:

You can meet all kinds of interesting people at the counter of Ellen's Coffee Shop in Chestertown. Slipping into a seat and grabbing a menu, I notice a lively conversation nearby. A slender dark-haired fellow is talking about trees. Curious, but not very familiar with the subject, I join in with a question, "Do you think oak is the best firewood?" I ask him. "Pretty much anything but pine," he says. "Oak, walnut, hickory, maple - but pine tar gets stuck in the chimney."

It turns out Jake Brown is a woodsman who grew up in Trappe, Maryland. He has worked all over the Eastern Shore cutting and trimming trees and seems particularly impressed with the beauty of big trees.

"Have you seen the giant sycamore in Easton – on Sycamore Lane?" he asks. "No, but I'd like to."

And, there's also, he adds, a very large willow I should look at, just a few blocks from here next to the Chester River Bridge.

While Brown goes on to speak highly of oaks, especially red oak with its reddish wood, and white oak for its light color, his favorite tree is the walnut. With its varying shades of cream, tan, brown and black, the range of color inside a walnut tree, says Brown, is unique. Living off Walnut Point Road in Chestertown, I can relate to his enthusiasm. Many tall, slender walnut trees with their long, narrow, elliptical leaves line the end of the street near my driveway.

Another popular tree with Brown is Osage orange.

"The wood is dense, really hard," says Brown, "and an amazing shade of yellow inside."

A friend of his uses it in making furniture, mostly benches and chairs for restaurants. It is also very suitable for boats since it is resistant to rot; Osage orange makes up the whole frame of the 18th century replica schooner *Sultana* built in Chestertown. Although it is usually a small tree, an enormous Osage orange stands outside the Miller Library at Washington College in Chestertown.

Delmarva produces quite a mix of good wood, according to Brown, including sycamore – although he's not that fond of sycamores. Says he's probably allergic to them. Their dangling puff ball-like fruit makes him sneeze.

I ask Brown about one of my favorite trees – white birch. Growing up in New England, I remember peeling back its papery bark, which revealed an even softer, smoother layer of bark underneath. It was fun, too, throwing white birch logs onto a fire and watching all the fireworks. Brown says he doesn't see much white birch on the Eastern Shore; it's a colder climate tree.

Also missing from Delmarva's tree-scape, though once quite visible, adds Brown, is the elm. Dutch elm disease, a fungus carried by bark beetles, killed huge numbers of elms. But he says elm seedlings resistant to Dutch elm disease are now being planted in some areas. As for the wood, it is strong and also good for boat building.

As 2 o'clock approaches and lunch hour winds down at Ellen's, I pay my bill and get ready to leave. I thank Jake Brown for being such good company at the counter. In just a short time, he has taught me a lot about trees and wood. I'll now be looking at trees a little differently – and with a lot more interest.

Postscript

Responses to this story are fun. A neighbor who now thinks I'm an expert on trees asks me to identify a huge one in his backyard. Luckily, it's a sycamore – one of the few trees I recognize. It's fun being considered an authority on something, especially when you're not!

Chesapeake Times sends over a letter addressed to me. It's from a woman asking if I've seen some of the "very old and lovely trees" at a nearby local church. I haven't, so I take a drive over to look, and find a huge towering oak. Wow. I write her back a note of thanks.

Then a family friend calls to tell me he read the article and wishes he'd been at the counter that day. He knows a lot about trees, especially the black walnuts that grow up all around us.

WOMEN ON WHEELS

After Motorcycle Safety Class I finally get in touch with the woman who emailed me about joining Women on Wheels (WOW). By now I'm thinking about writing an article on women and motorcycling. Hearing that a group of WOW members will be riding up the Eastern Shore of Maryland and stopping for lunch at Waterman's Restaurant in nearby Rock Hall, I ask if I can join them. Would I like to ride my motorcycle with the group and then have lunch? a member replies. Looking out at my bike sitting in the garage with a dead battery, flat tire and another problem yet to be determined reminds me that motorcycle maintenance is not my forte. So, I have to decline her invitation to ride. We agree to meet at Waterman's.

Arriving at the restaurant in my Volvo station wagon – a poor substitute for my Honda 250 Rebel – I set up in the parking lot so when the women ride in, I can snap pictures.

Here's how I wrote it for "Delmarva Quarterly" magazine.

Women on Wheels

The region's flat roads and great scenery beckon growing legions of women who enjoy riding together.
By Mary Saner

At a low rumble, the line of motorcycles circles into the lot outside Waterman's Restaurant in Rock Hall, Md. Atop, wearing helmets and clad in bright colors, the drivers slowly move their bikes up side by side, cutting their engines. It is the first stop on an Eastern Shore ride for the Delmarva Lady Cruisers. Wearing a big smile, and first to take off her helmet is Jennifer Williams, who's 56 and a lawyer from Easton. She's riding a Yamaha 1300 (that's a large motorcycle).

"I was looking for women to ride with, people who were very supportive as I was kind of getting my feet wet," says Williams, who joined the Lady Cruisers – a local chapter of the national organization, Women on Wheels (WOW) – right after getting her motorcycle license four years ago.

A couple of bikes down in the straight row of shiny motorcycles is Debbie Moore, 48, who removed her leather jacket. Underneath, a sequined motorcycle on her white T-shirt glitters in the sun. When she's not running an architectural firm, competing in ice dancing or teaching archery, Moore says she loves to ride. "There's a feeling of freedom, the camaraderie of being with people who enjoy the same thing."

Moore, Williams and their fellow riders are part of a nationwide trend – the huge increase in motorcycle driving, especially among women. According to recent statistics, women motorcyclists have increased about 40 percent in the last decade. Now, as many as four and a half million women in the U.S. operate motorcycles – many having started as passengers. And, while California claims the most motorcycles, Maryland, Delaware and Virginia are proving to be popular biking territory.

The Delmarva Lady Cruisers are partial to the Eastern Shore with its flatness, few big curves and many great water views. Driving in the lead position today on her BMW 1200, Lisa Strang describes the beauty of Delmarva biking. "In order to ride safely, you really have to be on top of your game and constantly scan what's ahead of you," says Strang. "It's amazing – while you're doing that scanning, you're taking in so much more, of the different shades of greens in the trees, or you ride by a magnolia tree or some honeysuckle, and it smells great."

While the Delmarva Lady Cruisers spend most of their time east of the Bay Bridge, they do take trips into Western Maryland and Pennsylvania. Gaby Rudderow, 54, rides her Honda 750 with a WOW chapter in Anne Arundel County, but often joins her Eastern Shore friends. Dressed in leather and denim, (the clothing of protection for motorcyclists), Rudderow says she wishes there wasn't an image problem for bikers. "A misconception is that there are a lot of them out there that just like to go bar hopping and make loud noises and be daring," says Rudderow. "But there's another whole side of it, about enjoying beautiful scenery and fresh air, which is exhilarating and has solitude at the same time. It's the thrill of the ride."

As the number of motorcyclists has grown, so, unfortunately has the incidence of biking accidents. While realistic about the dangers involved, the Lady Cruisers strongly defend their pastime. Amanda Longfellow, who's ridden 33 years and whose mother rode a motorcycle in the Army during World War II, speaks with confidence while aboard her Honda 1500. "There's always risk. I'm more worried for the people on the road than I am for myself. I know what my capabilities are. I know how much time and space I need for my bike to stop – what space I can maneuver my bike through, what terrain I don't want to take my bike on," says Longfellow. Fellow rider, Rudderow, who has taken long trips on her motorcycle, including a six-day ride to Quebec and back, says safety is a key part of biking. "There's a lot you can do to be safe – be very defensive. When the light turns green, that's not just a signal to go, it's a signal to look both ways. When you stop, you have to be aware of your surroundings all the time. We wear as much protective clothing as we can and be comfortable, abide by the law, and just be very aware."

Trying to get together at least once a month for a ride – oftentimes for charity – the group also tries to gather for a monthly social event like lunch or dinner. Through it all, the Delmarva Lady Cruisers say they've developed a special bond that's tied to self-confidence, encouragement, friendship and an absence of pressure. Rudderow, whose leather vest features a long row of WOW badges for mileage milestones and recruiting new members, says this fellowship is a very important part of her life. "You can be riding out west and see the logo and know that's a sister, that's a family member, that you have a lot in common with, that you can sit right down with them and chat with them about experiences you've had, places you've been. You probably even know some of the same people. It's the journey, the camaraderie that does it for me."

WOW had more than 3500 members in 75 chapters through the country. The Delmarva Lady Cruisers are headquartered in Salisbury.

Delmarva Quarterly   Autumn
2007

GLIMPSES OF A FEW MORE RADIO FEATURES

Nicknames

In the fishing town of Rock Hall, Maryland, watermen go by nicknames like "Buffalo," "Eel," "Shortcake" and "Termite." Many of my friends think this story idea is funny. My nephew thinks that Shortcake is a particularly good nickname. By the time I've finished interviewing, the nickname phenomenon doesn't seem that odd to me anymore. How watermen have earned their nicknames makes a lot of sense.

They may have been earned – or given – in childhood, but Rock Hall watermen usually keep their nicknames for life – and those names tell something special about them.

Don "Dog" Pierce got his nickname years ago while working on his fishing boat during a stretch of good weather. Another waterman remarked that he was doggin' his crew to death. But when the weather turned bad and nobody could fish, Dog tells me his crew had money in their pockets. He says he often works like a dog.

I interview "Pie" Edwards on his back porch on Piney Neck Road in Rock Hall. Pie, who's 83, is a retired waterman with a long family history in Rock Hall. He's not sure where he got his nickname, but says he got it early, maybe because his face was pie-shaped or because he liked to eat pie. He says his father who was a redhead went by "Red Oak" and his uncles "White Oak" and "Hemlock." All three men were tough, Pie adds.

Pie knows everyone in town and introduces me to "Buddy" Elburn, who's very friendly, and "Trapper" Thomas, who's known as one of the area's best animal trappers. I feel like I've known them all for a long time.

"Can you give me a nickname?" I ask Pie at the end of the interview. "Miss Sally," he says without hesitation. When I ask why he chose that, he only smiles. No explanation necessary. I like the name and use it in my byline.

Produced for Voice of America and Westwood One Radio Network

Bay Bridge Blues

A lot of people are afraid to drive across bridges, particularly ones that are long and high. A driving service at the Chesapeake Bay Bridge takes people across the Bay who are afraid of driving across themselves. In taping this show I'm in the backseat of the car hanging over the front seat holding up my microphone between Susan Jimenez, who has gephyrophobia (a fear of bridges) and is sitting on the passenger side, and Skip Morgan, a supervisor for the Vehicle Recovery Team who's at the wheel of Susan's car.

As Bernie Adams told me all those years ago during my internship when I asked him how close I need to be with my mic to record someone's voice clearly, he said, "Close enough to smell their breath." While it's not very technical, I get the picture and get close enough to Jimenez and Morgan to gather good sound.

What makes the story work is that Susan Jimenez vividly tells why she fears bridges. She describes a bad fall she took from a second story while in her 20's that broke her hip and arm. Now she fears flying off the end of suspension cables when she approaches them on bridges.

What might help Ms. Jimenez and others, says a Bay Bridge official, is to walk across the bridge during an event called "Bridge Walk." Being surrounded by people while seeing the bridge from a different perspective might ease anxiety.

Produced for Westwood One Radio Network and Voice of America

Music Therapy

R arely in producing a show do I ever feel emotional. Maybe it's because I'm so busy with questions and recording and everything else that's going on. But with this program, the pain and suffering that cancer has inflicted on children is right before my eyes. In recording the kids as they play drums, bells, tambourines, and maracas despite the plastic tubes that attach some of them to an IV stand, I clearly see and hear their spirit. But there is one girl who does not respond to my questions. She is sitting in a wheelchair with a faraway look in her eyes. She is not trying at all to participate in the music session. This is the first time I remember stopping all efforts for an answer. She does not want to talk and I could not bear to force her.

Produced for Voice of America

Organic Farmer

I meet Dolly Baker in 2001 while producing a video with friends about the old house where Dolly lives. Legend has it that a ghost lives there, too – has been a resident there for more than 200 years. Dolly doesn't deny it. She tells us about all the strange sounds she hears in the house, not just the normal old house sounds, but things like footsteps on the stairs – when no one else is home.

I learn that Dolly was once a marine biologist and botanical illustrator but switched careers at the millennium to become an organic farmer. I'm interested in producing a story about organic farming on the Eastern Shore of Maryland and Dolly's happy to share her experiences with me.

We agree to meet at Dolly's place (the one with the ghost). It's called White House Farm. The house was built by her ancestors in 1721 and is now listed on the National Register for Historic Places. A few miles north of Chestertown, the white brick house sits on a hill surrounded by rich farmland.

For the interview Dolly and I sit down beside an old empty swimming pool. Grass is growing up between the cracks in the concrete under our feet. There's a picket fence behind us covered in overhanging vines. I feel close to nature here – figuratively and literally.

Dolly says that anyone can claim to grow all-natural produce, but she abides by strict rules for government organic certification – like no fungicides or other chemicals; natural fertilizers only. She must keep log books, too, that document composting and other activities. It's hard work being certified, she says.

She grows over 100 varieties of organic tomatoes and collects heirloom tomato seeds (hence her nickname "Tomato Lady"). In wintertime Dolly turns her kitchen into a makeshift greenhouse. Small white cups cover the counter; she fills each of them with a mixture of five organic tomato seeds and organic soil. As the seeds grow, she separates them into larger cups, then in the early spring puts the plants into frames and sets them out by the pool. Come mid-April, they're for sale at the Farmers Market in Chestertown. Dolly grows other vegetables, too, raises chickens and sells eggs, and raises turkeys – a rare breed called "Black Spanish Turkeys." Fenced in close to the house, they're making a racket.

"I'm cutting back 'cause the beasts are big and they're always knocking me down in the mud," she says, laughing.

Produced for Voice of America

The Thatcher

I arrive one Saturday morning at a house on Long Island to interview a thatcher. He's building a new roof there using a reed called phragmites, which is an invasive species in many wetland areas in the eastern U.S.

My story line seems simple. Colin McGhee is a master thatcher from England who is growing a business in America where thatch was once used by early settlers in the 1600's. But rarely are stories simple or easy. For starters, McGhee's nine-year old son has come along to work with him. Right away I'm thinking about the role he will play in this piece. He is already busy separating the piles of phragmites on the ground into smaller batches for carrying up the ladder to the roof. He tells me he also carries tools up there and water for his father.

But McGhee keeps his son off the roof for now. It's steep, slippery and partially covered in a thick mat of reeds that McGhee has attached to a lattice-like framework. McGhee says phragmites is waterproof, fireproof and very durable – lasting fifty to sixty years on a roof. But building with it is expensive because of the hours of labor and cost of materials. It can take a month or longer to do a roof, he says, rather than the usual one or two days. And, there is no market for phragmites in the U.S. – so no one harvests it. McGhee gets the reed for this job from China.

McGhee has a job scheduled this year in Nashville. Tim McGraw and Faith Hill want him to put a thatched roof on their new home. It would be fun to follow him south for some interviews and produce another show for a different network. But for now, I have my story here on Long Island and am now thinking, too, about a possible sequel. There might be an interesting story one day about a Father & Son business that's reviving the art of building with thatch in America.

Produced for Voice of America

Postscript

Living in the small town of Chestertown, I have friends in many different professions. When finding facts for stories, I sometimes call a friend. For this feature, I need a second opinion on how long it takes to build a traditional shingle roof. So, I call a friend and neighbor across Langford Creek, Mike Taylor, who owns a building and contracting business in Chestertown. He confirms immediately: a day or two. Thanks Mike, I'm glad I know you!

STORY IDEAS COME AND GONE

A lot of story ideas don't make it to the airwaves for one reason or another. Here are a few of those.

Fried Ants

Eating insects is common in some countries. But when I mention this story idea to a producer of a morning show, he tells me listeners won't want to hear about eating insects at breakfast time.

The Art of Whistling

Whether making music or conversing with birds, a whistler needs to perfect certain skills. How about a whistling festival in Maryland that features technical skills for music and bird calling? This story idea fizzles out when two editors lose interest.

BerkShares

BerkShares is a local currency that began in Great Barrington, Massachusetts and spread to several other towns in the Berkshire Hills. Banks issue BerkShares for use at local businesses in an effort to boost local economies. To produce this show I'd need to be in Massachusetts. Travel expenses discourage me from following up.

White-Nose Syndrome

White-Nose Syndrome (WNS) has killed a massive number of bats in the U.S., mostly in the northeast. Researchers believe a fungus is involved, but that the fungus may be only a symptom of a bigger problem. WNS has spread from caves in New York to ones in Massachusetts, Connecticut, Vermont, Pennsylvania, New Jersey and most recently West Virginia and Virginia. When hibernating, infected bats have what looks like white powder on their noses and wing membranes.

Researchers think that something disturbs the bats during hibernation. When awakened and flying, they burn up fat reserves and eventually die of malnourishment. Some environmental groups suspect that cavers may be spreading WNS in their clothing and gear. As a result, many caves are now gated. Cavers are being warned to disinfect clothes and boots with bleach before exploring an open cave.

I am in touch with a biologist in the Maryland Department of Natural Resources who works in western Maryland near the border with West Virginia – a state recently found to have WNS. He offers to take me inside a cave located a few miles from his house. But the visit is delayed. I forget the reasons why. I never make it into the cave.

Epilogue

Over the years I've produced a lot of radio features. Too many to count. I have interviewed hundreds of people in my work. Each one has taught me something interesting, and something I can pass on to many others. Hopefully, with the publication of this book I will hear from some of you and we can continue the conversation.

--Mary Saner

Acknowledgements

I would like to thank Buzz Saner, Nancy Taylor Robson and Shelley Lepter. Without their help, this book would not have been possible.

Riding high at Elkhorn Ranch in Montana